AF332986

PUBLIC HEALTH IN THE 21ST CENTURY

OCCUPATIONAL SAFETY AND HEALTH

PUBLIC HEALTH IN THE 21ST CENTURY

Additional books in this series can be found on Nova's website
under the Series tab.

Additional e-books in this series can be found on Nova's website
under the e-book tab.

CONTENTS

PREFACE

Occupational safety and health (OSH) is broadly charged with the protection of the safety and health of people engaged in work while they are in the work environment. This may also include individuals associated with the workers (e.g., family), the profession (e.g., co-workers, employers) and the community (e.g., customers, providers) who may be affected by the safety and health characteristics of the work environment. The importance of occupational safety and health has been recognized as early as the 19th century and has been the subject of many labor movements, rules and laws across the world. Because occupational safety and health is directly associated with the well-being and quality of life of workers, there are moral, financial and legal rights, responsibilities and implications.

The occupational safety and health involves the integration of many disciplines including chemistry, biology, physics, engineering, medicine, ergonomics, hygiene, psychology, economics and law. Such as, occupational safety and health plans typically rely on a structured multi-level approach in which components of each individual discipline are merged in a dynamic model. The ability of the occupational safety and health plans to evolve is an essential component due to ever-lasting changes in community, social, financial, technological, health and political determinants on a local and an international scale. These changes also have a two-way effect. For example, many well-studied occupational chemical hazards are eliminated due to changes in manufacturing/processing activities, while other chemical compounds, for which the potential safety and health impacts are poorly characterized, are introduced.

The globalization of world economy, rapid technological advancements, new organizational and financial models and the rapid industrialization of developing and low-income countries with poor, if any, occupational safety and health laws and plans present major challenges to occupational safety and health as new hazards and risks are generated faster than the ability of existing occupational legislation and infrastructure to identify, prevent, control and/or mitigate them.

Given the vast range of disciplines in occupational safety and health matters, a single book cannot capture and describe all the different aspects as they evolve over time and around the world. In this book, we concentrated on specialized topics covering three domains: (i) chemical hazards; (ii) workload management and (iii) occupational education. We also provide insights in occupational safety and health aspects in different intellectual and cultural environments, highlighting the coupling between occupational safety, health and the community at-large.

Editors:

Ilias G. Kavouras, PhD
Associate Professor
Department of Environmental and Occupational Health
Fay W. Boozman College of Public Health
University of Arkansas for Medical Sciences
Little Rock, Arkansas 72205, USA

Marie-Cecile G. Chalbot, PhD
Instructor
Department of Environmental and Occupational Health
Fay W. Boozman College of Public Health
University of Arkansas for Medical Sciences
Little Rock, Arkansas 72205, USA

In: Occupational Safety and Health
Editors: I.G. Kavouras, M.C.G. Chalbot © 2014 Nova Science Publishers, Inc.

ISBN: 978-1-63117-695-1

Chapter 1

NANOTECHNOLOGY IN OCCUPATIONAL SAFETY AND HEALTH

Luc Fontana and Carole Pelissier
University of Jean Monnet and University Hospital,
Saint-Etienne, France

ABSTRACT

Nanotechnology is the manipulation of matter on an almost atomic scale to produce new structures, materials, and devices. As potential occupational exposure to nanomaterials (NMs) becomes more prevalent, it is important that the principles of medical surveillance and risk management be considered for workers in the nanotechnology industry. However, much information about health risk is beyond our current knowledge. Thus, NMs present new challenges to understanding, predicting, and managing potential health risks. First, we briefly describe some general features of NMs and list the most important types of NMs. This review discusses the toxicological potential of NMs by comparing possible injury mechanisms and known, or potentially adverse, health effects. We review the limited research to date for occupational exposure to these particles and how a worker might be exposed to NMs. The principles of medical surveillance are reviewed to further the discussion of occupational health surveillance for workers exposed to NMs. We outline how occupational health professionals could contribute to a better knowledge of health effects by the utilization of a health surveillance program and by minimizing exposure. Finally, we discuss the early steps towards regulation and the difficulties facing regulators in controlling potentially harmful exposures in the absence of sufficient scientific evidence.

INTRODUCTION

Nanoparticles are defined as particles that have at least one dimension <100 nm. Nanoparticles are ubiquitous in nature, naturally occurring as by-products of wild fires, volcanic eruptions, and other natural processes, usually called ultra-fine particles. Nanoparticles can also be a result of human activities unintentionally produced and present in polluting emissions, such as welding fumes, cigarette smoke, aircraft waist gas, or diesel exhaust, also called ultra fine particles. In additional to these sources, a number of artificial nanoparticles, which exhibit unique physical, chemical and/or biological characteristics associated with their nanostructure, have recently been developed and produced in a controlled, engineered manner to exploit their novel properties and functions. Many nanotechnology applications are based on novel as well as conventional materials deliberately engineered to be nanostructured, for which the term "nanomaterial," or "nanoobjects," is now frequently used (Lövestam et al., 2010). In 2011, the European Commission adopted the following definition: 'Nanomaterial' (NM) means a natural, incidental, or manufactured material containing particles, in an unbound state or as an aggregate or as an agglomerate and where, for 50 % or more of the particles in the number size distribution, one or more external dimensions is in the size range 1 nm-100 nm (European Union, 2011). Nanotechnology is the creation and/or manipulation of particles at a nanometre scale to produce new structures, materials, and devices, in many different technological areas and industrial sectors. To date, nanotechnology represents a rather broad interdisciplinary field of research and industrial activity. Some of these engineered nanomaterials (NMs) are already in use in consumer products. NMs are increasingly being used for commercial purposes, and in the future, more workers will come in contact with NMs. As we said, such materials possess nanostructure-dependent properties (e.g., chemical, physical, biological), which make them desirable for commercial or industrial applications. However, these same properties may potentially lead to atypical toxicity. Thus, concerns about the potential risks of exposure to humans have been raised. As potential occupational exposure to NMs becomes more prevalent, it is important that the principles of medical surveillance and risk management be considered for workers in the nanotechnology industry. However, much information about toxicity and health risk is beyond our current knowledge. Thus, NMs present new challenges to understanding, predicting, and managing potential health risks. In this review, intentionally-manufactured nanoscale materials will be referred to as NMs.

The goals of this review are to describe some general features of NMs, present a partial overview of current data on nanotoxicology and on some potential health effects, describe how a worker might be exposed to NMs, report the limited research to date for occupational exposure to these NMs, and relate the principles of hazard prevention in the workplace, such as medical surveillance.

THE NANOMATERIALS, APPLICATIONS AND USES

Nanomaterials are usually produced by bottoms-up processes, such as physical and chemical vapor deposition, liquid phase synthesis, and self-assembly (Bergamaschi E, 2009; Yokel and MacPhail, 2011). Currently, there is not a widely used, standardized nomenclature for NMs. They are usually classified based on their morphology (Aitken et al., 2004). Nanoscale particles can be tubular (nanotubes), spherical, irregularly shaped, and may also exist in aggregated formations (dendrimers). Generally, the most common NMs types are fullerenes, carbon nanotubes, quantum dots, metal nanoparticles, nanowires, nanoporous materials, metal oxide/ceramic nanoparticles, and nanofibers (Aitken et al., 2004; Aitken et al., 2006). Fullerenes are comprised entirely of carbon and take the form of hollow spheres or tubes. The smallest fullerene, termed buckminsterfullerene (familiarly referred to as buckyballs), is the most familiar and recognizable from of nanoparticles addressed in common and scientific literature.

Nanotubes are actually comprised of fullerene-like (carbon) particles that are elongated to form tubular structures having a diameter of 1 to 2 nanometers. Carbon nanotubes have a lot of highly useful properties such as great tensile strength, capacity for high conductivity, and high molecular absorption. Sometimes referred to as artificial atoms, quantum dots are assemblies of materials between 2 to 10 nanometers. They can be composed of metals, metal oxides, or semiconductor materials and typically exhibit unconventional electronic, magnetic, optical, or catalytic properties. These particles are termed "quantum dots," because their final size (alone) can control their physical properties.

Metal nanoparticles are produced from metals, especially gold and silver. Nanowires are, essentially, tiny interconnecting wires of a single crystalline structure constructed using approaches similar to semiconductor fabrication – template disposition. Some of them are produced from silicon, cobalt, gold, or copper. Nanoporous materials are defined as those porous materials with pore diameters less than 100 nm. They offer new opportunities in areas of inclusion chemistry, guest-host synthesis, molecular manipulations, and reactions on the nanoscale for making nanoparticles, nanowires, and other quantum nanostructures. Porous materials can be classified according to their constituents (such as organic or inorganic; ceramic or metal) or their properties. Today, the most commercially important nanomaterials are simple metal oxides, such as silica, titania, alumina, iron oxide, zinc oxide, ceria, and zirconia. Also, of increasing importance are mixed oxides, such indium-tin oxide and antimony-tin oxide, silicates, and titanates. Other types of nanoparticles, including various complex oxides, semiconductors, nonoxide ceramics (e.g., tungsten carbide) and metals are also under development and available from some companies in laboratory- and pilot-scale quantities. Finally, nanofibers are defined as fibers with diameters in the nano scale. Some materials regarded as NMs have been on the market for a long time.

The well known NM, carbon black, was used in industrial production over a century ago. In 1915, it was introduced as a reinforcing agent for the production of car tires. Nanowerk identified ~2500 commercial NMs, including ~27% metal oxides, 24% carbon nanotubes, 18% elements, 7% quantum dots, and 5% fullerenes (Nanowerk, 2012a). The Nanotechnology Products and Applications database provides an overview of how NMs and nanostructuring applications are used today in industrial and commercial applications across industries: chemicals; commodities; construction (building materials, glass, insulation, paint, wear protection, steel…); energy sector (fuel cells, gas turbines, solar cells, wind turbines, light emission …); environment (carbon capture, drinking water filtration, waste water treatment…); food (food packaging, food processing); electrical engineering; machinery (insulation, lubrication, protective garments); information and communications technology (data storage, displays, electronics, optics and photonics); medicine (antimicrobial, dental, diagnostics, drug delivery, implants, pharmaceuticals, therapeutics); precision engineering (coatings, metrology, optics); textiles and garments; transportation (Nanowerk, 2012b). NMs are also present in consumer products (cosmetics and personal care products, household products, medical & healthcare products). They are primarily composed of silver, carbon, zinc, silica, titanium, and gold (Yokel and MacPhail, 2011).

A considerable number of new NMs are constantly being developed and introduced. Nanoscale products and materials are increasingly being used in optoelectronic, electronic (e.g., computer hard drives), magnetic, medical imaging, drug delivery, cosmetic and sunscreen, catalytic, stain resistant fabric, dental bonding, corrosion-resistance, and coating applications (O'Brien and Cummins, 2009). Major future applications are expected to be in motor vehicles, electronics, personal care products and cosmetics, and household and home improvement products.

Toxicity

Available data on the toxicology of NMs are mainly from in vitro or laboratory animal studies. Epidemiological data is limited for occupational exposure to NMs. Presently, there is only limited knowledge. However, it is now known that the toxic behavior of nanoparticles differs from their bulk counterparts. Even nanoparticles that have the same chemical composition differ in their toxicological properties; the differences in toxicity depend upon size, shape, and surface covering (Kumar et al., 2012). There are strong indications that these properties are responsible for observed responses in cell cultures and animals (CDC, 2012). Animal toxicology literature describes a variety of toxicological effects from exposures to specific types of nanoparticles. In vitro and in vivo studies have revealed that most nanoparticles are toxic to animals.

Nanoparticles that have been studied are titanium dioxide, alumina, zinc oxide, carbon black, carbon nanotubes, and "nano-C60." Dose, route of administration, and exposure are critical factors that affect the degree of toxicity produced by any particular type of NM (Kumar et al., 2012). However, because the characteristics of exposure and the route of administration in these studies are often different from potential workplace exposures, and the dose is often larger, one cannot assume that findings in these studies would apply to humans exposed in occupational settings. More experimental evidence is required to determine whether in vitro data are relevant to effects observed in vivo and how to translate these data into a predicted response in humans.

Routes of Exposure

The principal routes of occupational NMs exposures are through the respiratory tract, by inhalation, the skin, by trans-dermal absorption, and the gastrointestinal tract, by ingestion (Aitken et al., 2006; Cormode et al., 2009; Tinkle et al., 2003; Maynard and Kuempel, 2005;

Borm et al., 2006). The nasal cavity and eyes are also cited (Kagan et al., 2010). The inhalation route has been of greatest concern and the most studied, because it is the most common route of exposure to airborne particles in the workplace. The skin has also been investigated. Most studies have shown little to no transdermal NM absorption. Oral (gastrointestinal) exposure can occur from intentional ingestion, unintentional hand-to-mouth transfer from inhaled particles > 5 μm that are cleared via the mucociliary escalator, and from drainage from the eye socket via the nasal cavity following ocular exposure. Direct uptake of nanoscale materials from the nasal cavity into the brain via the olfactory and trigeminal nerves has been shown (Yokel and MacPhail, 2011).

Routes that avoid first-pass clearance and metabolism in the gastrointestinal tract and liver include uptake (absorption) from the nasal cavity (either into systemic circulation or directly into the brain), orotransmucosal (e.g., buccal [from the cheek] and sub-lingual), and transdermal. These routes may present a greater risk of NMs-induced adverse effects because more NM is likely to reach the target organ(s) of toxicity (Yokel and MacPhail, 2011).

Toxicokinetics

A few studies have investigated the pharmacokinetics of NMs in whole animals, including absorption, distribution, metabolism, and excretion patterns at the systemic level. NMs can gain access to the blood stream via inhalation and dermal exposure (Oberdörster et al., 2005; Hoet et al., 2004; Wang et al., 2012). Then, once in the blood stream, due to the small size of NMs, they can be transported throughout the circulation around the body and be taken up by organs and tissues, including the brain, heart, liver, kidneys, spleen, bone marrow, and nervous system (Oberdörster et al., 2005). Some types of nanoparticles have been shown to escape normal lung clearance processes (alveolar macrophage phagocytosis) (Donaldson et al., 2001) and enter the lung interstitium to a greater extent (Donaldson et al., 2001; Mercer et al.,

2010; Mercer et al., 2011). Current studies suggest that multiple factors control the circulation and organ clearance of NMs. A nanoparticle's interaction with plasma proteins and blood components may influence uptake and clearance and, hence, potentially affect distribution and delivery to the intended target sites. There have been preclinical studies to understand nanoparticle interaction with the immune system and its potential effects on nanoparticle biodistribution (Kumar et al., 2010; Dobrovolskaia et al., 2008). Moreover, the size, shape, surface charge, surface functional groups, and aspect ratio of NMs, as well as tissue microstructures, strongly influence the circulation of NMs in bloodstream, their site-specific extravasation, and their clearance profiles within organs (Wang et al., 2012). Because of their large surface area, NMs, on exposure to tissue and fluids, will immediately absorb onto their surface some of the macromolecules they encounter (Kunzmann et al., 2011).

The mechanism of cellular uptake of nanoparticles may occur through several different pathways, depending on the properties of the nanoparticles but also on the specific cell type in question. Furthermore, the interaction between cells and nanoparticles is influenced by plasma proteins, which have been shown to coat nanoparticles instantly upon contact with plasma (Kunzmann et al., 2011; Nel et al., 2009). Moreover, as particles are mainly recognized and engulfed by immune cells, special attention should be paid to nano–immuno interactions. Nano–immuno interactions are, therefore, important to consider when engineered NMs are devised for in vivo administration (Dobrovolskaia et al., 2008; Kunzmann et al., 2011; Dobrovolskaia and McNeil, 2007). NMs are able to cross biological membranes and access cells (probably by phagocytosis for nanoparticles more than 1 µm and by diffusion for nanoparticles less than 1 µm), tissues, and organs that larger-sized particles normally cannot (Holsapple et al., 2005). The small size of NMs facilitates not only uptake into cells and invasion into many tissues, once incorporated into the body, but also penetrates nuclei (Hackenberg et al., 2010). The metabolism of many NMs has not been studied in detail. Most metabolic studies on NMs have employed traditional analytical methods to compare results from nanoscale with non-nanoscale materials. It is difficult to detect and quantify the metabolism of NMs by a single analytical technology. Specific characteristics of nanoparticles may require additional considerations of methodologies to measure the unique features of the distribution and metabolism of nanoparticles (Liang et al., 2008). After exposures, significant accumulations of NMs have been found in the lungs, brain, liver, spleen, and bones of test species (Wang et al., 2012).

The persistence of NMs may be a major factor contributing to their effects. Many NMs are designed to be mechanically strong and resist degradation (Yokel and MacPhail, 2011; 16). Referring to nanoscale fiber-like structures, it has been stated: "The slower [they] are cleared (high bio-persistence) the higher is the probability of an adverse response" (Dekkers et al., 2006). The prolonged physical presence of NMs that are not metabolized or cleared by macrophages or other defence mechanisms appears to elicit ongoing cellular responses. The majority of carbon nanotubes is assumed to be biopersistent (Yokel and MacPhail, 2011). The persistence of NMs in tissue raises justifiable concerns about their potential to cause long-term or delayed toxicity. NMs excretion depends on the route of exposure. After inhalation, nanomaterials are slowly eliminated (Deng et al., 2007). Nanomaterials in blood can be filtered through the kidneys and excreted in the urine (Ruggiero et al., 2010). After ingestion, nanomaterials are not absorbed in the gastrointestinal tract and are excreted directly via the feces (Deng et al., 2007). But, in some cases, biliary excretion may play a role. However, nanomaterials accumulated in aggregate forms, mainly in liver, are eliminated from these organs via slow hepatobiliary excretion (Baek et al., 2012; Georgin et al., 2009). Smaller particles were cleared more rapidly than larger ones.

Toxicodynamics

The available data on NMs toxicity is yet limited. NMs have produced an array of different toxic effects in many different types of in vivo and in vitro studies. The animal toxicology literature describes a variety of toxicological effects from exposures to specific types of NMs (Nanoparticle Task Force ACOEM, 2011). In vitro and in vivo studies on NPs have revealed that most are toxic to animals. Several physico-chemical parameters have been proposed as critical determinants in NM toxicity: size, shape, surface functionalization or coating, solubility, surface reactivity (ability to generate reactive oxidant species), association with biological proteins (opsonization), binding to receptors, and, importantly, their strong tendency to agglomerate, but no single parameter has yet been identified as responsible for toxicity (Kumar et al., 2012). The very small size distribution and large surface area of NMs that are available for reaction might play a significant role in nanotoxicity.

Most of the experimental studies have involved a limited set of more common NMs, such as carbon black, metal oxide NPs (titanium dioxide, iron oxide), amorphous silica, carbon nanotubes (CNTs), and certain other carbon

NMs. Yet, very little is known about their interactions with biological systems (Yokel and MacPhail, 2011; Nanoparticle Task Force ACOEM, 2011). Common findings of many studies include induction of inflammatory processes and oxidative stress. However, correlation between responses of cells in culture and in vivo models is often low (Warheit DB et al., 2009; Jones and Grainger, 2009). NMs have proved toxic to human tissue and cell cultures, resulting in increased oxidative stress, inflammatory cytokine production, apoptosis of various human cell lines, and cell death (Oberdörster et al., 2005). Unlike larger particles, NMs may be taken up by cell mitochondria and the cell nucleus and induce major structural damage to mitochondria, even resulting in cell death (Li et al., 2003; Monteiro-Riviere et al., 2005; Porter et al., 2007; Geiser et al., 2005; Savic et al., 2003). Exposure of BEAS-2B cells to 15- to 45-nm ceria or 21-nm titania resulted in an increase of reactive oxygen species (ROS), increased expression of inflammation-related genes, induction of oxidative stress-related genes, induction of the apoptotic process, decreased glutathione, and cell death (Park et al., 2008). Twenty-nm ceria increased ROS generation, lipid peroxidation, and cell membrane leakage, and decreased glutathione α-tocopherol (vitamin E) and cell viability in a human bronchoalveolar carcinoma-derived cell line (A549) (Lin et al., 2006). Various metal oxides differentially inhibited cell proliferation and viability, increased oxidative stress, and altered membrane permeability of human lung epithelial cells (Kim et al., 2010). Exposure of a cell line derived from normal human bronchial epithelial (BEAS-2B) cells to some NMs produced genotoxicity and decreased cell viability (Lindberg et al., 2009).

The greater chemical reactivity of NMs can result in increased production of ROS, including free radicals. ROS production has been found in a diverse range of NMs including carbon fullerenes, carbon nanotubes, and nanoparticle metal oxides. ROS and free radical production is one of the primary mechanisms of nanoparticle toxicity; it may result in oxidative stress, inflammation, and consequent damage to proteins, membranes, and DNA (Nel et al., 2006). The respiratory tract and lungs are considered the primary target organ for inhaled NMs and NMs are more likely to be toxic than the same materials of conventional sized samples and can be inhaled more deeply into the lungs (Bakand et al., 2012). Animal studies with lung-derived cells in culture have documented adverse pulmonary effects, for example: pulmonary inflammation with granuloma formation and diffuse fibrosis after respiratory exposure (inhalation or intratracheal instillation) (Kelly, 2009). Inhaled NMs might have the potential to aggravate existing respiratory conditions such as asthma or bronchitis (Oberdörster, 2001).

While the respiratory tract is considered the primary target organ for inhaled NMs, there is translocation from the lung towards other organs for some NMs (Hoet et al., 2004; Ma et al., 2010). Specific consequences of this translocation are largely unknown. However, preliminary results indicated that affected organ systems may show inflammation, including the brain, altered heart rate and functions, and oxidative stress acute mitochondrial DNA damage, atherosclerosis, distressed aortic mitochondrial homeostasis, accelerated atherogenesis, increased serum inflammatory proteins, blood coagulation, hepatotoxicity, eosinophil activation (suggesting an allergic response), release of IL-6 (the main inducer of the acute phase inflammatory response), and an increase of plasminogen activator inhibitor-1 (a pro-coagulant acute phase protein) (Yokel and MacPhail, 2011; Hoet et al., 2004; Wang et al., 2008; Borm et al., 2006). Some animal studies have demonstrated translocation from the nasal cavity to the brain via the olfactory nerve (Wang et al., 2008). Ingested NMs may be absorbed through the intestinal lining and translocate into the blood stream where they undergo first pass metabolism in the liver (Yokel and MacPhail, 2011). Again, the effects of this translocation are largely unknown.

Dermal uptake is limited and does not appear to produce systemic effects (Borm et al., 2006). However, one study has demonstrated the ability of metal oxide NMs to produce dermatotoxicity (Samberg et al., 2010). NMs have the physical-chemical characteristics, such as size, shape, surface properties, to result in genotoxic interactions and interact with DNA, and thus, have potential to promote DNA damage or cancer. Many of the genotoxic effects associated with NMs (mainly with titanium dioxide and of carbon black NMs) may be directly related to the characteristics of the nanoparticle surface: functionality, charge, and induced charge (Oberdörster et al., 2005). In vitro and in vivo studies demonstrate the potential for NMs to cause and to produce genotoxic DNA mutation (Geiser et al., 2005; Lindberg et al., 2009). Carbon-based NMs produced pro-inflammatory, oxidative-stress, and genotoxic effects (Monteiller et al., 2007; Totsuka et al., 2009; Landsiede et al., 2009). Carcinogenicity data on nanoparticles are limited. Some studies have shown that certain NMs, cause lung tumor development in rats following inhalation (Kolling et al., 2008; Baan, 2007). Mesothelioma induction was also observed in mice exposed to NMs (NIOSH, 2009). In summary, NMs may have genotoxic and carcinogenic potential, but inconsistencies in the literature cause difficulties in drawing firm conclusions.

HEALTH EFFECTS

One may differentiate:

- fixed nanoparticles are incorporated into a substance, material, liquid, or device (nanocomposites, nanostructured surfaces, and nanocomponents) (electronic, optical, sensors, etc.);
- free nanoparticles are present at some stage in production or use individual nanoparticles.

These free nanoparticles could be nanoscale species of elements or simple compounds but also complex compounds where, for instance, a nanoparticle of a particular element is coated with another substance.

Occupational health risks might be associated with manufacturing and using NMs and with using (processing, etc.) materials containing nanoparticles that may be detected. Thus, workplace exposure to engineered NMs might not be confined to the initial manufacturing processes such as research or production processes, but might also occur during maintenance or modification activities, such as handling, machining, cutting, sanding, or drilling, that may disrupt the manufacture of finished products or components fabricated with NMs. At the present time, material safety data sheets and other safety information that accompanies finished products may not reliably indicate the presence of engineered NMs. There seems to be a consensus that, although one should be aware of materials containing fixed NMs, the immediate concern is with free NMs. Powder or liquid containing NMs are almost never monodispersed, but will contain a range of particle sizes. NMs show a tendency to aggregate, as in welding fumes and black carbon, and such aggregates often behave differently from individual nanoparticles (Aitken et al., 2004). The site of deposition and potential for absorption after inhalation exposure will be affected by the agglomeration of NMs in air. The most extensive exposures to NMs likely occur in the workplace, particularly research laboratories; start-up companies; pilot production facilities; and operations where NMs are processed, used, disposed, or recycled (Brouwer, 2010). Workers who use NMs may be unintentionally exposed, through inhalation, dermal contact, or ingestion, depending upon how employees use and handle them. The most likely route of exposure to NMs in an occupational setting would be by inhalation, as is true for other airborne particles (Yokel and MacPhail, 2011). Processes that lead to airborne nanometer-diameter particles, respirable nanostructured particles (typically smaller than 4 μmeters), and respirable droplets of NM suspensions, solutions, and slurries are of particular concern for potential inhalation exposures. However, no conclusive data on effects on workers' health of exposure or use of NMs exists. One may cite a case report, published in 2009, which described the results of 7 young Chinese females exposed to nanoparticles without any protective measures for 5–13 months, causing shortness of breath and pleural effusions (Song et al., 2009). Pathological examinations of patients' lung tissue displayed nonspecific pulmonary inflammation, pulmonary fibrosis, and foreign-body granulomas of the pleura. Using transmission electron microscopy, nanoparticles were found lodged in the cytoplasm and caryoplasm of pulmonary epithelial and mesothelial cells, but were also located in chest fluid (Song et al., 2009). Another case report has been published about a female open office worker who developed weight loss and diarrhea (Theegarten, et al., 2010). Laparoscopy performed for suspected endometriosis surprisingly revealed black spots within the peritoneum (Theegarten, et al., 2010). Submesothelial aggregates of carbon nanoparticles were found by scanning and transmission electron microscopy in these tissue specimens (Theegarten, et al., 2010). There is sparse knowledge as to the likelihood, frequency, and intensity of exposures experienced by those working around engineered nanoparticles. Similarly, there is little knowledge regarding the potential existence, type, and dose dependence of adverse health effects that might result from workplace exposures to engineered nanoparticles (Nanoparticle Task Force ACOEM, 2011).

In the occupational context, hazard identification can be re-stated as "What effects do NMs have on workers' health?" to which the National Institute for Occupational Safety and Health (or NIOSH) has stated: "No conclusive data on engineered nanoparticles exist for answering that question, yet. Workers within nanotechnology-related industries have the potential to be exposed to uniquely engineered materials with novel sizes, shapes, and chemical properties, at levels far exceeding ambient concentrations...much research is still needed" (NIOSH, 2009a). Although toxic effects have not been really demonstrated in humans, there is accumulating evidence from experimental studies that exposure to some NMs may be harmful (Nanoparticle Task Force ACOEM, 2011). However, it is mostly based on animal experiments with questionable relevance of routes of administration that are often different from potential workplace exposures such as intratracheal instillation of nanoparticle-containing solutions with larger dosing and cell culture-based in vitro experiments. One cannot assume that the findings in these studies would apply to humans exposed in occupational settings (Yokel and MacPhail, 2011).

One cannot always predict NM toxicity from the known effects of bulk or solution NM components. Similarly, the effects produced by NM components do not reliably predict NM effects (Priester et al., 2009). Thus, potential effects on human health depend on the specific physical and chemical properties of NMs and also on the mode of entry (oral, respiratory, dermal) and the way the body will manage the NM (target organs, metabolism, elimination, and effects observed).

The knowledge of ultrafine-particle health effects has been applied to NMs. One source of data on the impact of small particle exposure is the research on air pollution and ultrafine particles (the size of particles less than 100 nm in diameter, produced unintentionally by combustion and similar processes). These particles have a similar size distribution to, though different composition than, engineered NMs (Nanoparticle Task Force ACOEM, 2011). Epidemiologic studies have evaluated health outcomes in populations environmentally exposed to particulate matter, including fine and ultrafine particles, as a result of air pollution. There is evidence from these studies for increased pulmonary and cardiac morbidity and mortality, such as from asthma and ischemic heart disease, related to increases in ultrafine particulate concentration. Studies of workers exposed to mixtures of fine and ultrafine particulates also have documented declines in pulmonary function and excesses of respiratory symptoms (Nanoparticle Task Force ACOEM, 2011; Ibald-Mulli et al., 2002; Hesterberg et al., 2010). However, the toxicity from ultrafine materials and NMs is not always the same (Madl and Pinkerton, 2009).

In summary, in the absence of specific human data, one may say that the toxicologic evidence to date, while not conclusive, is relevant for humans, suggesting that workers exposed to NMs may be at some risk. The respiratory tract, and specifically the alveolar (gas-exchange) region, is the main target for the deposited dose of respirable particles including nanoparticles. Because of their properties, one may also say that inhaled or ingested NMs can cross biologic barriers and translocate to some organs. But, the toxic behavior of nanoparticles in humans remains one of the big issues that need to be resolved. How do they interact physiologically and chemically with the body's systems? Will those interactions be harmless, or could they cause acute or chronic adverse effects?

PREVENTION IN WORKPLACE

Exposure Assessment

While exposures to NMs in occupational settings are likely to fall below mass-based exposure limits, conventional assessment of hazard, based on such limits, may not be relevant to (or protective for) NMs. NMs, like ultrafine particles, have very low mass relative to larger particles. Measurements of mass concentration ($\mu g/m3$) are likely to be low, despite high particle number concentrations. Thus, gravimetric workplace exposure limits that apply to large particles may not be adequately protective when applied to NMs of the same material. Therefore, it is difficult to make recommendations for exposure assessment methodology. The optimal methods for exposure assessment of engineered NMs will likely be different from those used in traditional industrial hygiene monitoring for large particles. Regarding exposure assessment, The National Institute for Occupational Safety and Health (NIOSH) recommends that "Regardless of the metric and method selected for exposure monitoring, it is critical that measurements be taken before production or processing of a nanomaterial to obtain background nanoparticle exposure data."

Risk Management

Because of uncertainty regarding the potential for human health effects from exposure to NMs in light of growing research data indicating adverse health effects in laboratory animals and given the lack of occupational exposure standards to provide guidance, the most prudent approach is to minimize exposure, as is done for harmful chemicals (Yokel and MacPhail, 2011). The goal in managing the potential risks from NMs is to minimize exposure. In the absence of specific information on NMs, the extensive scientific literature on airborne, respirable aerosols and fibers has been used to develop interim guidance for working safely with NMs (EHS.MIT, 2012).

Engineering Controls

The potential for exposure to NMs, influenced by the quantity used and the form in which NMs occur, should be considered in designing appropriate controls. NM exposure can be reduced or completely eliminated through the use of engineering controls, such as: process changes, material containment, and enclosures operating at negative pressure compared to the worker's breathing zone; worker isolation; separated rooms; the use of robots; and local exhaust ventilation with a high efficiency particulate air filtration. Process/source enclosures (i.e., isolating the NM from the worker) can be aided by glove boxes, chemical fume hoods, biological safety cabinets, or an externally-vented local exhaust ventilation system. However, one should also consider that these methods can release NMs into the environment, potentially creating environmental pollution and loss of costly material (Yokel and MacPhail, 2011). A "down flow" booth, "elephant trunk," or fume hood may not provide sufficient protection because they may cause turbulence, spinning the NM out of the airflow (Tsai et al., 2010).

Personal Protective Equipment (PPE)

The last line of defense in the hierarchy of exposure control is the use of PPE such as respirators, protective clothing, and gloves (Yokel and MacPhail, 2011). Even though the need for respiratory protection for all NMs has not been established, respirators may be used to help reduce risk by lowering exposure to NMs. Selecting the appropriate respirator includes knowing the assigned protection factor needed, the filtration efficiency, and the face seal leakage. The sizes of NMs that may have the greatest effects in people are probably those best able to penetrate filtering face piece respirators. However, until results are obtained from clinical-laboratory or work-place studies, traditional respirator selection guidelines should be used. No guidelines are available on the selection of clothing or other apparel (e.g., gloves) for the prevention of dermal exposure to NMs. This is due, in part, to the minimal data available on the efficacy of existing protective clothing, including gloves. However, NIOSH also indicates that it is prudent to consider the use of protective clothing and gloves to minimize dermal exposure, although there are no scientific data from which to select the most effective protective equipment. Although nonwoven fabrics were much more effective to protect workers from NM exposure than woven fabrics, they are much less comfortable to wear, suggesting improvements in fabric design or selection are needed to address this disincentive to use more effective PPE. The selection of laboratory coat materials can greatly influence the potential penetration of NMs, which may end up on or penetrating street clothing, resulting in worker absorption or even greater dispersion into the environment (Ahn et al., 2005). An unpublished study reported that latex and nitrile gloves exhibited micrometer-sized surface pores/intrinsic voids, and there were wider gaps between the fibers in cotton gloves. They may serve as pathways for the penetration of nanoparticles under unfavourable conditions, such as stretching and tearing (Yokel and MacPhail, 2011). Stretching latex and nitrile gloves to 200% of their original size greatly increased the pores/intrinsic voids. Surface pores may be important if they collect nanoparticles and the user does not remove the gloves when going to another location, thereby transporting the NMs. Nitrile, latex, and neoprene gloves prevented ~10 nm titania and platinum ENM penetration (Golanski et al., 2010). Double gloving has been suggested, which should reduce material penetration when there is glove perforation as well as dermal contamination when removing a contaminated outer glove (Ahn et al., 2005). However, double gloving has not been shown to significantly decrease material penetration (Korniewicz et al., 1994).

Administrative Controls

When engineering controls are not feasible for reducing exposure, administrative controls should be implemented. These are policies and procedures aimed at limiting worker exposure to a hazard (Halperin, 1996). These could include a nanoscale material hygiene plan; preparation, training in, and monitoring use of standard operating procedures; reduction of exposure time; modification of work practices and respect of good work practices; and good workplace and housekeeping practices. Employee training in safe work practices, information regarding exposure controls, and potential NMs risks are also important (Nanoparticle Task Force ACOEM, 2011).

Medical Surveillance

Secondary prevention in the continuum of the prevention and hierarchy of exposure control includes biological monitoring and medical examination, the early detection of asymptomatic disease, and prompt intervention when the disease is preventable or more easily treatable (Halperin, 1996). Occupational health surveillance is the process by which information obtained from any activity in the continuum of prevention and hierarchy of exposure control is collected and used to support or alter what is done at a step higher in the hierarchy (Trout and Schulte, 2010).

Occupational health surveillance is the ongoing systematic collection, analysis, and dissemination of exposure and health data on groups of workers for the purpose of early detection and injury. It includes hazard surveillance, the periodic identification of potentially hazardous practices or exposures in the workplace, assessing the extent to which they can be linked to workers, the effectiveness of controls, and the reliability of exposure measures. A goal is to help define effective elements of the risk management program for exposed workers. Occupational health surveillance also includes medical surveillance, which examines health status to determine whether an employee is able to perform essential job functions (Yokel and MacPhail, 2011). The current NIOSH recommendation regarding medical surveillance for workers potentially exposed to nanoparticles states: "Currently there is insufficient scientific and medical evidence to recommend the specific medical screening of workers potentially exposed to engineered nanoparticles" (NIOSH, 2009b).

Nonetheless, this lack of evidence does not preclude specific medical screening by employers interested in taking precautions beyond existing industrial hygiene measures (Nanoparticle Task Force ACOEM, 2011). If nanoparticles are composed of a chemical or bulk material for which medical screening recommendations exist, these same screening recommendations would be applicable for workers exposed to engineered nanoparticles as well (NIOSH, 2009b). Because the human health effects, if any, from workplace NM exposure are unknown, appropriately targeted and specific medical surveillance programs cannot be defined at this time. Furthermore, it is uncertain whether screening methods commonly used in medical surveillance will have the sensitivity and specificity to detect potential early adverse effects from exposure to NMs.

In spite of these difficulties and uncertainties, two NIOSH scientists have recently recommended that a basic medical surveillance program be considered for groups of workers exposed to nanoparticles for which toxicology data suggest that there might be a risk of disease in exposed individuals (Nanoparticle Task Force ACOEM, 2011; NIOSH, 2009b). For NMs composed of materials for which there are already medical surveillance recommendations, NIOSH suggests that this screening would be applicable for those working around NMs. NIOSH suggests considering the use of exposure registries to identify workers exposed to NMs, which would permit longitudinal follow-up and, if appropriate, examination of these cohorts for the presence of findings or diseases that may be associated with their exposures.

The third level in the continuum of prevention and hierarchy of exposure control, tertiary prevention, includes diagnosis, therapy, and rehabilitation. Owing to the lack of documented episodes of ENM exposure in humans that have resulted in adverse outcome, there is little experience with treatments of ENM exposure.

Regulation

NMs are regulated by REACH (Regulation on Registration, Evaluation, Authorisation and Restriction of Chemicals), because they are covered by the definition of a chemical "substance" in REACH. The general obligations in REACH, therefore, apply as for any other substance, and there are no provisions referring explicitly to NMs (European Commission). The U.S. Environmental Protection Agency (EPA) is developing a Significant New Use Rule (SNUR) and other regulations to address potential health and environmental risks from nanoscale materials (USEPA). The U.S. NIOSH has published interim guidelines for working with NMs (Managing the Health and Safety Concerns Associated with Engineered Nanomaterials) and has created a Nanotechnology Field Research Effort to "assess workplace processes, materials, and control technologies associated with nanotechnology and conduct on-site assessments of potential occupational exposure to a variety of NMs" (UnderstandingNano).

The U.S. Food and Drug Administration (FDA) has the responsibility to review many types of new products such as food additives and pharmaceuticals. They have summarized their stance on nanotechnology and such products in the report FDA Regulation of Nanotechnology Products. The FDA has also released a draft document that, when finalized, is intended to "to help industry and others identify when they should consider potential implications for regulatory status, safety, effectiveness, or public health impact that may arise with the application of nanotechnology in FDA-regulated products" (UnderstandingNano).

Canada has regulations to ensure that any new substance being manufactured in Canada or imported into Canada undergoes a risk assessment of its potential effects on the environment and human health. Environment Canadian has issued guidelines to help determine if a NM is considered a new substance (UnderstandingNano).

CONCLUSION

Despite recent progress in research, understanding of the potential health effects of engineered NMs or products incorporating NMs is still incomplete and, in particular, the long-term effects are, as yet, still unknown. Currently, there are insufficient data to permit the conduct of risk assessments for individual types of NMs, with limitations affecting each step of the risk assessment process (Nanoparticle Task Force ACOEM, 2011). Needed information is lacking regarding the appropriate exposure metric, regarding exposure data from workplace settings, and regarding toxicity data, including dose–response information and information regarding absorption, distribution, metabolism, and excretion. There is also a need for techniques and equipment to permit practical and appropriate exposure monitoring in workplaces.

At this time, the limited evidence available on health effects suggests caution when potential exposures to NMs may occur. Current recommendations to minimize hazards and exposure are largely based on common sense, knowledge by analogy to ultrafine material toxicity, and general health and safety recommendations. This is accomplished through effective application of engineering controls and personal protective equipment as part of a risk management program. Key questions concerning working with NMs include the following: Are workers being protected? Are we effectively translating the research findings into workplace practice? Are occupational health guidance and standards keeping pace with the development of new NMs? Are we effectively communicating the health risks and protective measures? (Kuempel et al., 2012). While the societal benefits of nanotechnology may be great, health safety issues must be given due attention (Crosera et al., 2009). Hence, there is great need for further research into nanotoxicology, the various aspects of occupational health and safety in nanotechnology.

REFERENCES

Ahn, K., Lee, J., Tsai, C., Mead, J., Ellenbecker, M. J. (2005). Use and efficacy of protective gloves in handling nanomaterials. Available from: http://www.turi.org/content/download/3270/29768/.../glove%20presentati on.pdf [accessed July 30, 2012]

Aitken, R. J., Chaudhry, M. Q., Boxall, A. B. A., Hull, M. (2006). Manufacture and use of nanomaterials: current status in the UK and global trends. *Occupational Medicine* 56, 300–306.

Aitken, R. J., Creely, K. S., Tran, C. L. (2004). Nanoparticles: An Occupational Hygiene Review. *HSE Research Report* 274. London: HSE Books.

Baan, R. A. (2007). Carcinogenic hazards from inhaled carbon black, titanium dioxide, and talc not containing asbestos or asbestiform fibers: recent evaluations by an IARC Monographs Working Group. *Inhalation Toxicology,* 19 Suppl 1, 213-228.

Baek, M., Chung, H. E., Yu, J., Lee, J. A., Kim, T. H., Oh, J. M., Lee, W. J., Paek, S. M., Lee, J. K., Jeong, J., Choy, J. H., Choi, S. J. (2012). Pharmacokinetics, tissue distribution, and excretion of zinc oxide nanoparticles. *International Journal of Nanomedicine*, 7, 3081-3097.

Bakand, S., Hayes, A., Dechsakulthorn, F. (2012). Nanoparticles: a review of particle toxicology following inhalation exposure. *Inhalation toxicology*, 24, 125-135.

Bergamaschi, E. (2009). Occupational exposure to nanomaterials: present knowledge and future development. *Nanotoxicology,* 2009, 3, 194-201.

Borm, P. J. A., Robbins, D., Haubold, S., Kuhlbusch, T., Fissan, H., Donaldson, K., Schins, R. P. F., Stone, V., Kreyling, W., Lademann, J., Krutmann, J., Warheit, D., Oberdorster, E. (2006). The potential risks of nanomaterials: a review carried out for ECETOC. *Particle and Fibre Toxicology* 3,11.

Borm, P. J., Robbins, D., Haubold, S., Kuhlbusch, T., Fissan, H., Donaldson, K., Schins, R., Stone, V., Kreyling, W., Lademann, J., Krutmann, J., Warheit, D., Oberdorster, E. (2006). The potential risks of nanomaterials: a review carried out for ECETOC. *Particle and Fibre Toxicology*, 3, 11.

Brouwer, D. (2010). Exposure to manufactured nanoparticles in different workplaces. *Toxicology,* 269, 120-127.

Centers for Disease Control and Prevention (CDC). (2012). Nanotechnology. Available from: http://www.cdc.gov/niosh/topics/nanotech/ [accessed July 30, 2012]

Cormode, D. P., Skajaa, T., Fayad, Z. A., Mulder, W. J. M. (2009). Nanotechnology in medical imaging: probe design and applications. *Arteriosclerosis, Thrombosis, and Vascular Biology*, 29, 992-1000.

Crosera, M., Bovenzi, M., Maina, G., Adami, G., Zanette, C., Florio, C., Filon Larese, F. (2009). Nanoparticle dermal absorption and toxicity: a review of the literature. *International Archives of Occupational and Environmental Health*, 82, 1043-1055.

Dekkers, S., de Heer, C., de Jong, W. H., Sips, A. J. A. M., van Engelen, J. G. M., Kampers, F. W. H. (2006). Nanomaterials in consumer products, Availability on the European market and adequacy of the regulatory framework. RIVM/SIR Advisory report 11014. European Parliament, Policy Department, Economic and Scientific Policy. Available from: http://www.europarl.europa.eu/comparl/envi/pdf/externalexpertise/nanom aterials_in_consumer_products.pdf [accessed July 30, 2012]

Deng, X., Jia, G., Wang, H., Sun, H., Wang, X., Yang, S., Wang, T., Liu, Y. (2007). Translocation and fate of multi-walled carbon nanotubes in vivo. Carbon, 45, 1419–1424.

Dobrovolskaia, M. A., Aggarwal, P., Hall, J. B., McNeil, S. E. (2008). Preclinical studies to understand nanoparticle interaction with the immune system and its potential effects on nanoparticle biodistribution. *Molecular Pharmaceutics*, 5, 487-495.

Dobrovolskaia, M. A., McNeil, S. E. (2007). Immunological properties of engineered nanomaterials. *Nature Nanotechnology*, 2, 469-478.

Donaldson, K., Stone, V., Clouter, A., Renwick, L., MacNee, W. (2001). Ultrafine particles. *Occupational and Environmental Medicine*. 58, 211-216.

EHS.MIT. Nanomaterials, toxicity. 2012 Available from: http://ehs.mit.edu/site/content/nanomaterials-use-reporting-instructions [accessed July 30, 2012]

European Commission. REACH and nanomaterials. Available from: http://ec.europa.eu/enterprise/sectors/chemicals/reach/nanomaterials/index _en.htm [accessed July 30, 2012]

European Union. (2011). Commission recommendation of 18 October 2011on the definition of nanomaterial. 20.10.2011. Available from: http://eur-lex.europa.eu/LexUriServ/LexUriServ.do?uri=OJ:L:2011:275:0038:0040: EN:PDF [accessed July 30, 2012]

Geiser, M., Rothen-Rutishauser, B., Kapp, N., Schürch, S., Kreyling, W., Schulz, H., Semmler, M., Im Hof, V., Heyder, J., Gehr, P. (2005). Ultrafine particles cross cellular membranes by nonphagocytic mechanisms in lungs and in cultured cells. Environmental *Heath Perspectives,* 113, 1555-1560.

Georgin, D., Czarny, B., Botquin, M., Mayne-L'hermite, M., Pinault, M., Bouchet-Fabre, B., Carriere, M., Poncy, J. L., Chau, Q., Maximilien, R., Dive, V., Taran, F. (2009). Preparation of (14)C-labeled multiwalled carbon nanotubes for biodistribution investigations. *Journal of the American Chemical Society*, 131, 14658-14659.

Golanski, L., Guiot, A., Tardif, F. (2010). Experimental evaluation of individual protection devices against different types of nanoaerosols: graphite, TiO2, and Pt. *Journal of Nanoparticle Research*, 12, 83-98.

Hackenberg, S., Friehs, G., Froelich, K., Ginzkey, C., Koehler, C., Scherzed, A., Burghartz, M., Hagen, R., Kleinsasser, N. (2010). Intracellular distribution, geno- and cytotoxic effects of nanosized titanium dioxide particles in the anatase crystal phase on human nasal mucosa cells. *Toxicology Letters*, 195, 9-14.

Halperin, W. E. (1996). The role of surveillance in the hierarchy of prevention. *American Journal of Industrial Medicine*, 29, 321-323.

Hesterberg, T. W., Long, C. M., Lapin, C. A., Hamade, A. K., Valberg, P. A. (2010). Diesel exhaust particulate (DEP) and nanoparticle exposures: what do DEP human clinical studies tell us about potential human health hazards of nanoparticles? *Inhalation toxicology*, 22, 679-694.

Hoet, P.H., Brüske-Hohlfeld, I., Salata, O. V. (2004). Nanoparticles - known and unknown health risks. *Journal of Nanobiotechnology*, 2, 12.

Holsapple, M. P., Farland, W. H., Landry, T. D., Monteiro-Riviere, N. A., Carter, J. M., Walker, N. J., Thomas, K. V. (2005). Research strategies for safety evaluation of nanomaterials, part II: toxicological and safety evaluation of nanomaterials, current challenges and data needs. *Toxicological Sciences*, 88, 12-7.

Ibald-Mulli, A., Wichmann, H. E., Kreyling, W., Peters, A. (2002). Epidemiological evidence on health effects of ultrafine particles. *Journal of aerosol medicine*, 15, 189-201.

Jones, C. F., Grainger, D. W. (2009). In vitro assessments of nanomaterial toxicity. *Advanced Drug Delivery Reviews*, 61, 438-456.

Kagan, V. E., Shi, J., Feng, W., Shvedova, A. A., Fadeel, B. (2010). Fantastic voyage and opportunities of engineered nanomaterials: what are the potential risks of occupational exposures? *Journal of Occupational and Environmental Medicine,* 52, 943-946.

Kelly, R. J. (2009). Occupational medicine implications of engineered nanoscale particulate matter. *Journal of Chemical Health Safety*, 16, 24-39.

Kim, I. S., Baek, M., Choi, S. J. (2010). Comparative cytotoxicity of Al2O3, CeO2, TiO2 and ZnO nanoparticles to human lung cells. *Journal of Nanoscience and Nanotechnology*, 10, 3453-3458.

Kolling, A., Ernst, H., Rittinghausen, S., Heinrich, U., Pott, F. (2008). Comparison of primary lung tumor incidences in the rat evaluated by the standard microscopy method and by multiple step sections. *Experimental and Toxicologic Pathology*, 60, 281-288.

Korniewicz, D. M., Kirwin, M., Cresci, K., Sing, T., Choo, T. E., Wool, M., Larson, E. (1994). Barrier protection with examination gloves: double versus single. *American Journal of Infection Control*, 22, 12-15.

Kuempel, E. D., Geraci, C. L., Schulte, P. A. (2012). Risk assessment and risk management of nanomaterials in the workplace: translating research to practice. *The Annals of Occupational Hygiene*, 56, 491-505.

Kumar, V., Kumari, A., Guleria, P., Yadav, S.K. (2012). Evaluating the toxicity of selected types of nanochemicals. *Reviews of Environmental Contamination and Toxicology*, 215, 39-121.

Kunzmann, A., Andersson, B., Thurnherr, T., Krug, H., Scheynius, A., Fadeel, B. (2011). Toxicology of engineered nanomaterials: focus on biocompatibility, biodistribution and biodegradation. *Biochimica et Biophysica Acta*, 1810, 361-373.

Landsiedel, R., Kapp, M. D., Schulz, M., Wiench, K., Oesch, F. (2009). Genotoxicity investigations on nanomaterials: methods, preparation and characterization of test material, potential artifacts and limitations--many questions, some answers. *Mutation Research*, 681, 241-258.

Li, N., Sioutas, C., Cho, A., Schmitz, D., Misra, C., Sempf, J., Wang, M., Oberley, T., Froines, J., Nel, A. (2003). Ultrafine particulate pollutants induce oxidative stress and mitochondrial damage. *Environmental Health Perspectives*, 111, 455–460.

Liang, X. J., Chen, C., Zhao, Y., Jia, L., Wang, P. C. (2008) Biopharmaceutics and therapeutic potential of engineered nanomaterials. *Current Drug Metabolism*, 9, 697-709.

Lin, W., Huang, Y. W., Zhou, X. D. Ma, Y.(2006). Toxicity of cerium oxide nanoparticles in human lung cancer cells. *International Journal of Toxicology*, 25, 451-457.

Lindberg, H. K., Falck, G. C., Suhonen, S., Vippola, M., Vanhala, E., Catalan, J., Savolainen, K., Norppa, H. (2009). Genotoxicity of nanomaterials: DNA damage and micronuclei induced by carbon nanotubes and graphite nanofibres in human bronchial epithelial cells in vitro. *Toxicology Letters*, 186, 166-173.

Lövestam, G., Rauscher, H., Roebben, G., Sokull Klüttgen, B., Gibson, N., Putaud, J. P., Stamm, H. (2010). Considerations on a Definition of Nanomaterial for Regulatory Purposes. Available from:http://ec.europa.eu

/dgs/jrc/downloads/jrc_reference_report_201007_nanomaterials.pdf [accessed July 30, 2012]

Ma, L., Liu, J., Li, N., Wang, J., Duan, Y., Yan, J., Liu, H., Wang, H., Hong, F. (2010). Oxidative stress in the brain of mice caused by translocated nanoparticulate TiO2 delivered to the abdominal cavity. *Biomaterials,* 31, 99-105.

Madl, A. K., Pinkerton, K. E. (2009). Health effects of inhaled engineered and incidental nanoparticles. Critical Reviews in Toxicology, 39, 629-658.

Maynard, A. D., Kuempel, E. D. (2005). Airborne nanostructured particles and occupational health. *Journal of Nanoparticle Research*, 7, 587–614.

Mercer, R. R., Hubbs, A. F., Scabilloni, J. F., Wang, L., Battelli, L. A., Schwegler-Berry, D., Castranova, V., Porter, D. W. (2010). Distribution and persistence of pleural penetrations by multi-walled carbon nanotubes. *Particle and Fibre Toxicology*, 7, 28.

Mercer, R. R., Hubbs, A. F., Scabilloni, J. F., Wang, L., Battelli, L. A., Friend, S., Castranova, V., Porter, D. W. (2011). Pulmonary fibrotic response to aspiration of multi-walled carbon nanotubes. *Particle and Fibre Toxicology*, 8, 21.

Monteiller, C., Tran, L., MacNee, W., Faux, S., Jones, A., Miller, B., Donaldson, K. (2007). The pro-inflammatory effects of low-toxicity low-solubility particles, nanoparticles and fine particles, on epithelial cells in vitro: the role of surface area. *Occupational and Environmental Medicine* 64, 609-615.

Monteiro-Riviere, N. A., Nemanich, R. J., Inman, A. O., Wang, Y. Y., Riviere, J. E. (2005). Multi-walled carbon nanotube interactions with human epidermal keratinocytes. *Toxicology letters*, 155, 377-384.

Nanoparticle Task Force ACOEM. (2011). Nanotechnology and health. *Journal of Occupational and Environmental Medicine*, 53, 687-689.

Nanowerk. (2012). Nanomaterial Database Search. Available from: http://www.nanowerk.com/phpscripts/n_dbsearch.php [accessed July 30, 2012]

Nanowerk. (2012). Nanotechnology Products and Applications. Available from: http://www.nanowerk.com/products/products.php [accessed July 30, 2012]

Nel, A. E., Mädler, L., Velegol, D., Xia, T., Hoek, E. M., Somasundaran, P., Klaessig, F., Castranova, V., Thompson, M. (2009). Understanding biophysicochemical interactions at the nano-bio interface. *Nature Materials,* 8, 543-357.

Nel, A., Xia, T., Mädler, L., Li, N. (2006). Toxic potential of materials at the nanolevel. *Science*, 311, 622-627.

NIOSH, 2009b. Current Intelligence Bulletin 60: Interim Guidance for Medical Screening and Hazard Surveillance for Workers Potentially Exposed to Engineered Nanoparticles. Department of Health and Human Services, Centers for Disease Control and Prevention, National Institute for Occupational Safety and Health. DHHS (NIOSH) Publication No. 2009–116. Available from: http://www.cdc.gov/niosh/docs/2009-116/pdfs/2009-116.pdf [accessed July 30, 2012]

NIOSH. 2009a. Approaches to safe nanotechnology. Managing the health and safety concerns associated with engineered nanomaterials. U.S. Department of Health and Human Services, Centers for Disease Control and Prevention, National Institute for Occupational Safety and Health. DHHS (NIOSH) Publication No. 2009–125. Available from: http://www.cdc.gov/niosh/docs/2009-125/pdfs/2009-125.pdf [accessed July 30, 2012]

O'Brien, N., Cummins, E. (2008). Recent developments in nanotechnology and risk assessment strategies for addressing public and environmental health concerns. *Human and Ecological Risk Assessment*, 14, 568-92.

Oberdörster, G. (2001). Pulmonary effects of inhaled ultrafine particles. *International Archives of Occupational and Environmental Health*, 74, 1-8.

Oberdörster, G., Maynard, A., Donaldson, K., Castranova, V., Fitzpatrick, J., Ausman, K., Carter, J., Karn, B., Kreyling, W., Lai, D., Olin, S., Monteiro-Riviere, N., Warheit, D., Yang, H. ILSI Research Foundation/Risk Science Institute Nanomaterial Toxicity Screening Working Group. (2005). Principles for characterizing the potential human health effects from exposure to nanomaterials: elements of a screening strategy. *Particle and Fibre Toxicology*, 2:8.

Oberdörster, G., Oberdörster, E., Oberdörster, J. (2005). Nanotoxicology: an emerging discipline evolving from studies of ultrafine Particles. *Environmental Health Perspectives*, 113, 823–839.

Park, E. J., Choi, J., Park, Y. K., Park, K. (2008). Oxidative stress induced by cerium oxide nanoparticles in cultured BEAS-2B cells. *Toxicology*, 245, 90-100.

Porter, A. E., Gass, M., Muller, K., Skepper, J. N., Midgley. P., Welland, M. (2007). Visualizing the uptake of C60 to the cytoplasm and nucleus of human monocyte-derived macrophage cells using energy-filtered transmission electron microscopy and electron tomography. *Environmental Science & Technology*, 41, 3012-3017.

Priester, J. H., Stoimenov, P. K., Mielke, R. E., Webb, S. M., Ehrhardt, C., Zhang, J. P., Stucky, G. D., Holden, P. A. (2009). Effects of soluble cadmium salts versus CdSe quantum dots on the growth of planktonic Pseudomonas aeruginosa. *Environmental Science & Technology*, 43, 2589-2594.

Ruggiero, A., Villa, C. H., Bander, E., Rey, D. A., Bergkvist, M., Batt, C. A., Manova-Todorova, K., Deen, W. M., Scheinberg, D. A., McDevitt, M. R. (2010). Paradoxical glomerular filtration of carbon nanotubes. *Proceedings of the National Academy of Sciences of the United States of America*, 107,12369-12374.

Samberg, M. E., Oldenburg, S. J., Monteiro-Riviere, N. A. (2010). Evaluation of silver nanoparticle toxicity in skin in vivo and keratinocytes in vitro. *Environmental Heath Perspectives*, 118, 407-413.

Savic, R., Luo, L., Eisenberg, A., Maysinger, D. (2003). Micellar nanocontainers distribute to defined cytoplasmic organelles. *Science,* 300, 615-618.

Schulte, P., Geraci, C., Zumwalde, R., Hoover, M., Kuempel, E. (2008). Occupational risk management of engineered nanoparticles. *Journal of Occuational and Environmental Hygiene*, 5, 239-249.

Song, Y., Li, .X, Du, X. (2009). Exposure to nanoparticles is related to pleural effusion, pulmonary fibrosis and granuloma. *European Respiratory Journal,* 34, 559–567.

Theegarten, D., Boukercha, S., Philippou, S., Anhenn, O. (2010). Submesothelial deposition of carbonnanoparticles after toner exposition: Case report. *Diagnostic Pathology*, 5, 77.

Tinkle, S. S., Antonini, J. M., Rich, B. A., Roberts, J. R., Salmen, R., DePree, K., Adkins, E. J. (2003). Skin as a route of exposure and sensitization in chronic beryllium disease. *Environmental Heath Perspectives*, 111, 1202-1208.

Totsuka, Y., Higuchi, T., Imai, T., Nishikawa, A., Nohmi, T., Kato, T., Masuda, S., Kinae, N., Hiyoshi, K., Ogo, S., Kawanishi, M., Yagi, T., Ichinose, T., Fukumori, N., Watanabe, M., Sugimura, T., Wakabayashi, K. (2009). Genotoxicity of nano/microparticles in in vitro micronuclei, in vivo comet and mutation assay systems. *Particle and Fibre Toxicology*, 6, 23.

Trout, D. B. (2011). General principles of medical surveillance: implications for workers potentially exposed to nanomaterials. Journal of Occupational and Environmental Medicine, 53, S22-S24.

Trout, D. B., Schulte, P. A. (2010). Medical surveillance, exposure registries, and epidemiologic research for workers exposed to nanomaterials. *Toxicology*, 269, 128-135.

Tsai, S. J., Huang, R. F., Ellenbecker, M. J. (2010). Airborne nanoparticle exposures while using constant-flow, constant-velocity, and air-curtain-isolated fume hoods. *The Annals of Occupational Hygiene*, 54, 78-87.

UnderstandingNano. Regulation of Nanotechnology Materials and Products. Available from : http://www.understandingnano.com/nanotechnology-regulation.html [accessed July 30, 2012]

US Environmental Protection Agency (EPA). Control of Nanoscale Materials under the Toxic Substances Control Act. Available from: http://www.epa.gov/oppt/nano/ [accessed July 30, 2012]

Wang, B., Xiao He, X., Zhang, Z., Zhao,Y., Feng, W.(2012). Metabolism of nanomaterials in vivo: blood circulation and organ clearance. *Accounts of Chemical Research*, Article ASAP.

Wang, J., Liu, Y., Jiao, F., Lao, F., Li, W., Gu, Y., Li, Y., Ge, C., Zhou, G., Li, B., Zhao, Y., Chai, Z., Chen, C. (2008). Time-dependent translocation and potential impairment on central nervous system by intranasally instilled TiO(2) nanoparticles. *Toxicology*, 254, 82-90.

Warheit, D. B., Sayes, C. M., Reed, K. L. (2009). Nanoscale and fine zinc oxide particles: can in vitro assays accurately forecast lung hazards following inhalation exposures? *Environmental Science & Technology*, 43, 7939-7945.

Yokel, R. A., MacPhail, R. C. (2011). Engineered nanomaterials: exposures, hazards, and risk prevention. *Journal of Occupational Medicine and Toxicology*, 6, 7.

In: Occupational Safety and Health   ISBN: 978-1-63117-695-1
Editors: I.G. Kavouras, M.C.G. Chalbot © 2014 Nova Science Publishers, Inc.

Chapter 2

ASSESSMENT OF TUNNEL NO_2 AND O_3 CONCENTRATIONS USING PASSIVE SAMPLERS: APPLICABILITY FOR OCCUPATIONAL EXPOSURES

Marie-Cecile G. Chalbot[1] and Spyros Lykoudis[2]
[1]College of Public Health,
University of Arkansas for Medical Sciences, Arkansas, US
[2]National Observatory of Athens, Athens, Greece

ABSTRACT

NO_2 and O_3 concentrations were monitored in four one-way road tunnels of the newly constructed Attiki Odos in the area of Athens, Greece using Radiello diffusive samplers. Differences among urban, street-level and tunnel concentration for both NO_2 and O_3 indicated the vital impact of traffic emissions. NO_2 levels grew along the tunnel (from 30.2 ± 3.1 µg/m^3) resulting in high concentrations near the exit (up to 90 µg/m^3), because of the poor ventilation and the piston-effect of traffic movement. Conversely, O_3 concentrations dropped from 39.2 ± 1.0 µg/m^3 to almost 1.5 µg/m^3, demonstrating the substantial effect of elevated traffic emissions on chemistry and oxidative content of tunnel air. Despite different traffic flows and tunnel length, regression analysis showed that NO_2 concentrations were proportionally related to the distance from the tunnel entry; whereas, a rather poor relationship was observed for ozone.

The results of this study indicated that the length of the tunnel, a tunnel-design parameter, could be used as a surrogate to monitor air quality even in short tunnels. In addition, passive samplers could be employed to measure the concentrations of NO_2 and O_3, even in extremely polluted environments such as road tunnels.

INTRODUCTION

Diesel exhaust is a known human carcinogen by the International Agency for Research on Cancer based on sufficient evidence in animals and humans. The human epidemiologic evidence rests largely on studies of lung cancer among truck drivers, bus drivers, dock workers and railroad workers exposed to diesel exhaust. Workers in the trucking industry have a 32 to 49% increased risk for heart disease and a 40% increased risk for lung cancer as compared to the general US population (Garshick et al., 1998, 2004; Steenland et al., 2003; Laden et al., 2007). Exposure of highway patrolmen to particulate matter was found to be associated with irregular heart rate and increases in blood inflammatory markers (Riediker et al., 2004). A meta-analysis on bladder cancer found an excess risk of 13% for those exposed to diesel exhaust (Bofetta and Silvermass, 2001; Goldberg et al., 2001). Traffic exhaust is a complex and variable mixture of gases, vapors and fine particles. The amount and composition of the exhaust vary greatly, depending on factors such as fuel and engine type, maintenance schedule, tuning and environmental conditions. The gaseous constituents include hydrocarbons and oxides of carbon, sulphur and nitrogen.

Road tunnels were commonly built to reduce traffic congestion in urban areas and due to topography in mountainous areas. Typical tunnel ventilation systems have included transverse (full or semi) or longitudinal ventilation.

Transverse ventilation has been typically used in long vehicle tunnels, while longitudinal ventilation, caused by the piston-action of the traffic, has been preferred because of lower construction and maintenance costs.

Due to tunnel low volumes and poor ventilation systems, pollutants remain in tunnels for long periods of time, resulting in high concentration levels. Air quality inside road tunnels has been considered lately, because of the adverse outcomes of elevated concentrations of traffic-related pollutants (Chang et al., 1981; DeFre et al., 1994; Gertler et al., 1996; Chan et al., 1996; Barrefors, 1996; McLaren et al., 1996; Pucher and Zwiener, 1997; Fraser et al., 1998).

Tunnel air quality characterization and modeling studies have also been done to estimate emission factors of traffic pollutants including particulate matter and volatile organic compounds because of the accurate monitoring of tailpipe and non-tailpipe emissions and limited effects of photochemical reactions (Gertler et al., 1006; Rogak et al., 1998).

In this study, measurements of NO$_2$ and O$_3$ concentrations have been carried out in tunnels in order to assess air quality inside road tunnels and implications on occupational exposures, local atmospheric chemistry and public health. Nitrogen dioxide (NO$_2$) has been used as a tracer of traffic-related emissions because of the strong correlation between NO$_2$ concentration and traffic characteristics such as traffic density and distance from the road (Roorda-Knape et al., 1999; Gilbert et al., 2003). Furthermore, O$_3$ was used to examine possible outcomes on atmospheric chemistry, because it is primarily formed through atmospheric oxidation reactions of nitrogen oxides (NO$_x$ = NO + NO$_2$) and volatile organic compounds (VOCs).

METHODOLOGY

This study was conducted in College and Demokritos Tunnels of the newly constructed Ymittos Western Peripheral motorway from September 29, 2003 to October 3, 2003. A diagram of the Attiki Odos and the city of Athens highway and national road network is illustrated in Figure 1. Attiki Odos highway, the newest high-speed toll motorway in the European Union (http://www.aodos.gr), opened for traffic in June 2003. It is incorporated in the Trans-European Network, and it is the backbone of the Athens transport network. It directly connects the city centre to the Athens International Airport "Eleftherios Venizelos" and to the seaports of Piraeus, Lavrio and Rafina and provides an *out-of-city* linkage of the two primary national highways in the country: the Athens-Thessaloniki highway and the Athens-Patras highway. It is comprised of two main highways: the Elefsina-Spata motorway (52.4 km) and the Ymittos Western Peripheral motorway (12.9 km) (Figure 1). Each direction consists of three traffic lanes and one emergency lane. There are thirty-two (32) multi-level interchanges connecting more than thirty (30) neighborhoods in the greater area of Athens and hundreds of over- and under-passes in order to relieve traffic congestion in major arteries. Almost one-quarter (15.6 km) of Attiki Odos is comprised of sixty-three (63) tunnels and cut-and-cover sections; most of these belong to the Ymittos Western Peripheral motorway which is located on the foot of Mt. Ymittos.

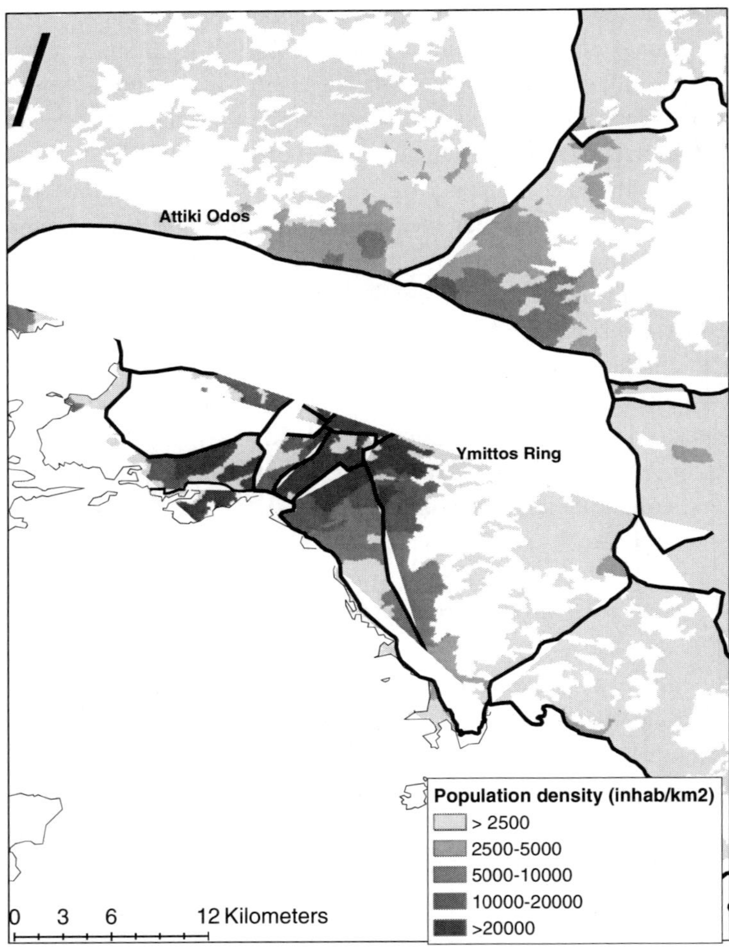

Figure 1. Schematic diagram of Attiki Odos including the Ymittos.

Each tunnel is composed of two one-way tubes with three traffic lanes of 5.5 meters wide. The length of the tunnels varied from 290 to 620 m (College: Northbound: 370 m; Southbound: 620 m and; Demokritos: Northbound: 290 m; South-bound: 450 m). The distance between the northbound and the southbound direction of each tunnel is ~ 6 meters. Ozone and nitrogen dioxide were measured with passive samplers at fifty-three (53) locations in and around the tunnels.

Radiello Model 3310 passive sampling systems for NO_2 and O_3, composed of coated collection bodies and cylindrical diffusive surfaces, were obtained from Rupprecht and Patashnick Co., Inc. (Albany, NY, US). Each set of passive samplers was installed 50 cm away from tunnel walls at a height of 1.8 m. The distance between passive samplers inside the tunnels was around 50.0 ± 0.5 m. In addition, samples were collected approximately 30 meters prior to the entry and after the exit of each tunnel. After collection, samplers were placed into pre-washed containers, wrapped with aluminium foil and stored at 4°C until analysis.

Standards of potassium nitrite (KNO_2) and 4-pyridine-carboxyaldehyde (C_6H_5NO) were obtained from Merck (Darmstadt, Germany) and Agros Chemicals (US), respectively. 2-Methyl-2-benzothiazolinon-hydrozone-hydrochloride (MBTH; $C_8H_{10}ClN_3S$), N-(1-napthyl)ethylene-diamide dihydrochloride (NEDA; $C_{12}H_{14}N_2$-2HCl) and sulphanylamide ($4\text{-}(NH_2)C_6H_4SO_2\,NH_2$) were obtained from Merck. Ultra pure water was produced using a reverse osmosis Millipore Direct-Q3 water purification system.

Gaseous NO_2 was absorbed on a collection body coated with a 20% aqueous solution of triethanolamine in the form of nitrite ion (NO_2^-). The Griess-Saltzmann reaction was performed in an aliquot of the extract. Briefly, ~ 0.5 ml of the extract was mixed with 5 ml of 1% w/v aqueous solution of sulpha-nylamide and 1 ml of 0.1% w/v of (N-(1-napthyl)ethyl diamine aqueous solution. The concentration of hydrazide was determined by spectrometry using a Chemito UV-2600 dual double-beam UV-vis spectrometer at 534 nm. The concentration of NO_2 (ppb) was calculated as follows:

$$C_{NO_2} = \frac{M_{NO_2}}{(1.78 \cdot 10^3 \cdot (273+\theta) - 0.349) \cdot t}$$

(1)

where M_{NO2} was the mass of nitrite in the extract (ng), t was the exposure time (min) and θ was the mean ambient temperature (°C).

Atmospheric ozone reacted with cis-4,4-pyridethylyne on silica gel to form 4-pyridine-carboxyaldehyde. From the stoichiometry of the reaction, 1 mg of ozone formed 4.46 µg of 4-pyridine-carboxyaldehyde. Silica gel was extracted with 5 ml of 0.5% w/v of 2-methyl-2benzothiazolinon-hydrozone-hydrochloride for 1 hour, and a yellow-colored hydrazide was formed. The concentration of hydrazide was determined by spectrometry using a Chemito UV-2600 dual double-beam UV-vis spectrometer at 430 nm. Ozone mean concentration is given by Equation 2.

$$C_{O_3} = \left(\frac{298}{273+\theta}\right)^{1.5} \frac{M_{O_3}}{Q_{O_3} \cdot t}$$

$$(2)$$

where M_{O3} was ozone mass (ng), t as the exposure time (min), θ was the mean ambient temperature (°C) and Q_{O3} is the sampling rate of ozone (ml/min).

The limit of detection (LOD) of the method was equal to three times the standard deviation of field blanks collected during the study. LOD for NO_2 and O_3 were 0.7 $\mu g/m^3$ and 0.6 $\mu g/m^3$, respectively. The lack of precision of passive samplers was compensated by using duplicate samples. The estimated coefficient of variance (%CV) (18.2% for NO_2 and 6.6% for O_3) indicated that passive samplers can quite accurately measure the concentration levels of air pollutants. Data was analyzed using SPSS software. Linear regression analysis was performed using both the distance and the logarithm of distance from the tunnel entry as independent variables. The dependent variable was the mean of NO_2 and O_3 results from each sampling location.

RESULTS AND DISCUSSION

The issue of air quality in road tunnels has been recently formulated and specific guidelines and threshold limits on ventilation and air pollution have been recommended (World Road Organization, 2000). Typical ventilation control systems were initially targeted on CO decrease in tunnels. Meanwhile, new fuel technology resulted in lower CO emissions, thus, new parameters of air quality including nitrogen dioxide (NO_2) and sulfur dioxide (SO_2), have been integrated into pollution and ventilation control strategies (Barrefors, 1996; World Road Organization, 2000).

Ambient and tunnel mean (standard deviation of the mean) NO_2 and O_3 concentrations are summarized in Table 1. In addition, concentration changes of NO_2 and O_3 at College (Figures 2a,c and 3b,d) and Demokritos (Figures 2a,c and 3b,d) tunnels are shown in Figure 2 and 3, respectively. The gray areas represent the length of each tunnel. During this study, tunnel NO_2 concentrations (from 30.2 ± 3.1 $\mu g/m^3$ to 64.5 ± 7.8 $\mu g/m^3$; Table 1) were below the threshold limit of 1 ppm for the protection of human health.

However, it is worthy to note that in-tunnel NO_2 concentrations increased nearly ten times as compared to the ambient concentrations in 600 meters under normal driving conditions, with no traffic congestion and average driving speed of 90 km/h (Figure 2).

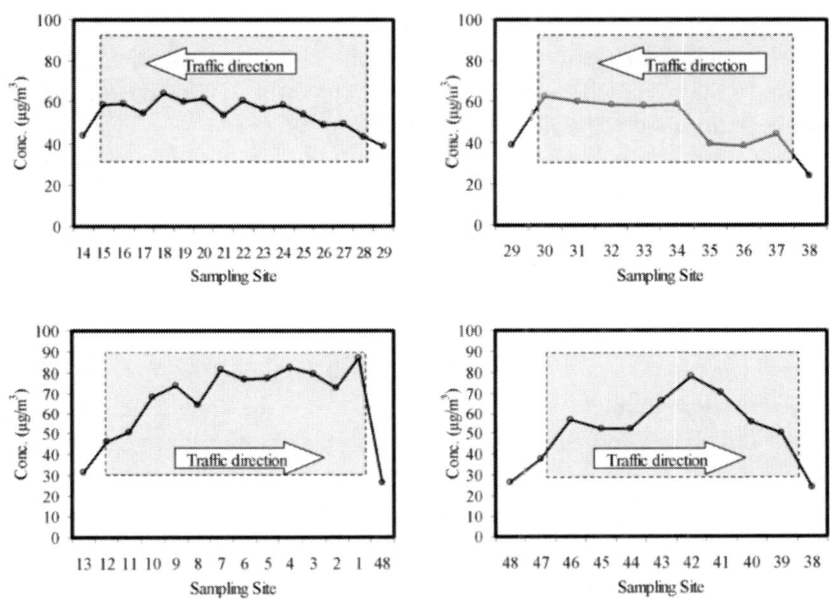

Figure 2. Concentration profiles of NO$_2$ (in µg/m^3) in College and Demokritos tunnels.

Thus, unexpected changes in traffic (e.g., congestions, car accidents and/or failure) may quickly aggravate NO$_2$ concentrations quite fast (Chan et al., 1996).

Atmospheric NO$_2$ and O$_3$ concentrations around the tunnels varied from 9.0 to 21.5 µg/m^3 (Mean: 12.3 ± 2.3 µg/m^3; Table 1) and from 58.7 to 73.1 µg/m^3 (Mean: 67.8 ± 2.6 µg/m^3; Table 1), respectively.

Conversely, higher NO$_2$ (from 30.2 ± 3.1 to 33.4 ± 4.7 µg/m^3; Table 1) and lower O$_3$ (from 43.5 ± 7.8 to 45.8 ± 6.3 µg/m^3; Table 1) concentrations were measured at the street level of tunnel entries (C_{i-1}) and exits (C_{j+1}). The in-tunnel concentrations of traffic-related NO$_2$ were up to three times higher than those measured at tunnel entries and up to eight times higher than those measured around tunnels. The increase was progressive (up to 90 µg/m^3; Figure 2c) with distance from the tunnel entry (Figure 2); however, the pattern was not similar for all tunnels.

A slower increase was observed for northbound (Figures 2a,b) than that for southbound tunnels (Figures 2c,d). In particular, mean NO$_2$ concentrations rose from 42.8 ± 1.8 $\mu g/m^3$ to 60.8 ± 4.4 $\mu g/m^3$ inside the tunnels, and up to 64.5 ± 7.8 $\mu g/m^3$ at the exit of the tunnel (Table 1). This was due to the piston effect caused by the movement of automobiles where air was pushed out of the tunnel along the direction of the traffic.

As a result, emissions accumulated along the length of the tunnels and gave rise to the highest levels at the exits (Chan et al., 1996l Barrefors, 1996; Funasaka et al., 1998; El-Fadel et al., 2000).

The modified NO_2 concentration trend in Demokritos tunnels (Figures 2 b,d) can be attributed to the penetration of wind into the tunnels (Bellasio, 1997). In fact, during the monitoring period, the prevailing wind direction was S-SW and the mean wind speed varied from 0.9 to 1.2 m/s. As a result, at the northbound tube, the growth of NO_2 was delayed and the southbound tunnel, accumulated NO_2 was diluted.

However, this was not possible for College tunnels because the distance between the two tunnels is short (< 50 m) and the height of the tunnels provided effective wind shading. These results suggested that ventilation was rather insufficient, irregular and non-continuous. For both north- and south-bound tunnels, NO_2 concentrations measured at the tunnel entry (30.2 ± 3.1 $\mu g/m^3$; Table 1) were comparable to those measured at the end of the tunnels (33.4 ± 4.7 $\mu g/m^3$; Table 1) pointing out that the high oxidation capacity of the atmosphere (e.g., high ozone) in the area did not tolerate important differences on air pollution levels before and after the tunnels.

An opposite profile was observed for tunnel O_3 concentrations. In fact, they decreased quickly from 39.2 ± 1.0 $\mu g/m^3$ to 14.4 ± 5.6 $\mu g/m^3$ inside the tunnels down to 6.4 ± 3.1 $\mu g/m^3$ at the exit of the tunnel (Table 1) presumably due to O_3 titration to NO_2 (Suppan et al., 2004).

Table 1. Ambient, street-level (C_{i-1}, C_{j-1}) and in-tunnel (C_{i+1}-C_{j-1}) mean ($\pm$ standard error) concentrations of NO_2 and O_3

	NO_2 ($\mu g\ m^{-3}$) *(Mean $\pm$ st. error)*	O_3 ($\mu g\ m^{-3}$) *(Mean $\pm$ st. error)*
Ambient	12.3 ± 2.3	67.8 ± 2.6
C_{i-1} (tunnel entry)	30.2 ± 3.1	45.8 ± 6.3
C_i	$42.8 \pm 1,8$	39.2 ± 1.0
C_{i+1} - C_{j-1}	60.8 ± 4.4	14.4 ± 5.6
C_j	64.5 ± 7.8	6.4 ± 3.1
C_{j+1} (tunnel exit)	33.4 ± 4.7	43.5 ± 7.8

Ozone concentrations declined quite quickly in southbound tunnels, while a gradual decrease was observed in northbound tunnels (Figures 3a,b). Lowest mean O$_3$ concentrations were measured just before the exits of southbound tunnels (~1.5 µg/m^3; Figures 3 c,d).

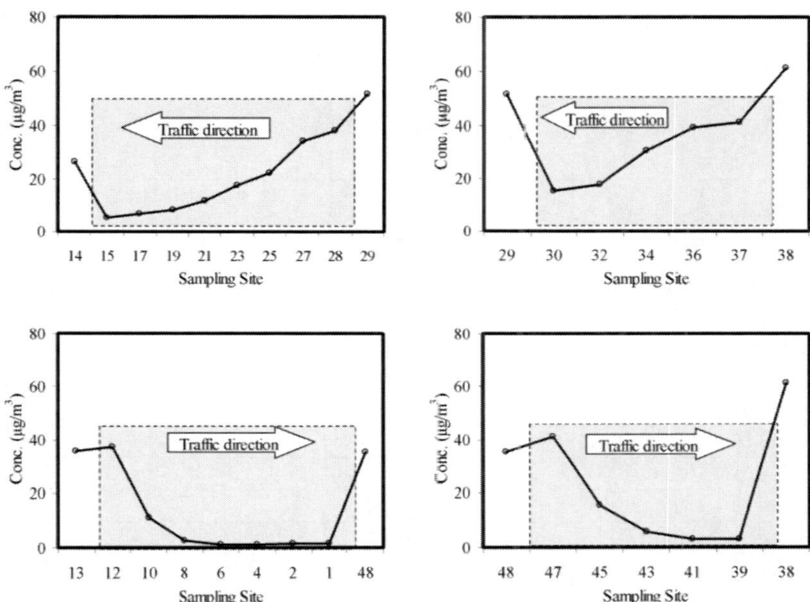

Figure 3. Concentration profiles of O$_3$ (in µg/m^3) in College and Demokritos tunnels.

In all cases, mean O$_3$ concentrations after tunnel exits (43.5 ± 7.8 µg/m^3; Table 1) were similar to those measured before tunnel entries (45.8 ± 6.3 µg/ m^3; Table 1). The possible effects of penetrating air in the Demokritos southbound tube on O$_3$ concentrations were not obvious, probably due to the fact that O$_3$ was consumed by high concentrations of NO$_x$.

The increase of NO$_2$ concentrations was linked to direct emissions of NO$_x$ from passenger cars, buses and heavy-duty cars. Previous studies (Funasaka et al., 1998; Indrehus and Vassbotn, 2001, 2001) have suggested that tunnel NO comprised 90% of NOx. As a result, chemical oxidation of NO with O3 was not feasible due to (i) high NO concentrations and (ii) extremely low O3 concentration encountered inside the tunnels. In addition, the so-called "thermal" conversion of NO with atmospheric oxygen was quite slow for ambient temperatures higher than 20°C (Indrehus et al., 2001).This observation was further supported by the strong linear relationship between tunnel NO2 concentrations and the distance from the tunnel entry.

Table 2 shows the linear regression model between NO_2 distance from the tunnel entry and O_3 concentrations and $\log_{10}$(distance) from the tunnel entry.

Table 2. Least-squares regression coefficients of NO_2 vs. distance from tunnel entry and O_3 vs log (distance from tunnel entry), in-tunnel measured and estimated mean concentrations and % root square mean error of NO_2 and O_3

Tunnel			p	R^2	Measured Conc.	Estimated Conc.	% RSME
			1. Nitrogen dioxide				
College-South	*Intercept*	41.16 ± 5.01	0.000	0.79	68.6 ± 4.5	74.4±5.9	18.7
(n=12)	*Slope*	0.11 ± 0.02	0.001				
College-North	*Intercept*	42.56 ± 2.40	0.000	0.74	54.8 ± 1.8	58.4±2.6	13.2
(n=14)	*Slope*	0.04 ± 0.01	0.003				
Demokritos-South (n=9)	*Intercept*	37.03 ± 6.54	0.001	0.6	54.5 ± 4.7	57.3±4.3	22.7
	Slope	0.09 ± 0.02	0.014				
Demokritos-North (n=8)	*Intercept*	32.01 ± 3.90	0.000	0.79	49.3 ± 4.4	49.3±3.9	11.3
	Slope	0.08 ± 0.01	0.001				
			2. Ozone				
College-South	*Intercept*	86.54 ± 15.71	0.002	0.69	8.1 ± 5.0	8.1 ±4.7	55.5
(n=7)	*Slope*	-32.33 ± 5.01	0.010				
College-North	*Intercept*	93.12 ± 13.22	0.000	0.87	18.1 ±4.4	18.1 ±4.3	8.3
(n=8)	*Slope*	-30.97 ± 6.01	0.000				
Demokritos-South (n=5)	*Intercept*	109.19 ± 15.48	0.003	0.81	13.7 ± 7.2	13.7 ± 7.0	23.4
	Slope	-41.63 ± 9.02	0.014				
Demokritos-North (n=4)	*Intercept*	95.76 ± 14.14	0.000	0.88	28.7 ± 5.2	28.7 ±4.9	11.6
	Slope	-30.24 ± 3.02	0.005				

A strong positive association between NO_2 and distance ($p<0.014$ and $R^2>0.60$; Table 2) was found. More specifically, the slope and the intercept varied from 0.04 ± 0.01 to 0.11 ± 0.02 and from 32.0 ± 3.9 to 42.5 ± 2.4 $\mu g/m^3$ (Table 2), respectively. Estimated mean NO_2 concentrations (from 49.3 ± 3.9 $\mu g/m^3$ to 74.7 ± 5.9 $\mu g/m^3$; Table 2) were always slightly higher (from 0 to 8.5%) than that measured using passive samplers concentrations (from 49.3 ± 4.4 $\mu g/m^3$ to 68.6 ± 4.5 $\mu g/m^3$; Table 2). The estimated % relative square mean error (% RSME) ranged from 11.3 to 22.7% (Table 2). The linear relationship between NO_2 and distance from the tunnel entry further provided evidence that a physical parameter, i.e., the length of the tunnel, can be used as a surrogate variable for NO$_2$. Similar results were also obtained in other studies where changes of in-tunnel concentrations are related to traffic volume, ventilation and tunnel length (Chan et al., 1996; El-Fadel et al., 2000).

A rather good linear relationship was found between ozone and log$_{10}$ (distance). The regression analysis of O$_3$ concentrations showed that both calculated slope and intercept were statistically significant (p<0.07). In addition, the estimated mean ozone concentrations (from 8.1 ± 4.3 µg/m^3 to 28.7 ± 4.9 µg/m^3; Table 2) were comparable to those measured in the tunnels (from 8.1 ± 5.0 µg/m^3 to 28.7 ± 5.2 µg/m^3; Table 2). %RSME values (from 8.28 to 55.5%; Table 2) indicated the correlation between ozone concentrations and the distance from the tunnel entry. These results revealed the drastic effect of elevated traffic emissions that altered both the oxidation capacity and chemistry in tunnels.

CONCLUSION

This study provides an initial indication of the exposures to nitrogen oxides of drivers and road construction workers. Considering the length of tunnels studied (less than 600 m), the estimated exposure time, under normal driving conditions (average speed of 80 km/h), of drivers and passengers was ca. >1.0 min. Indeed, the exposure time in tunnels was short; however, high NO$_x$ concentrations might have an impact on exposure levels (Barrefors, 1996). In fact, assuming that in-tunnel NO$_2$ / NO$_x$ = 0.1, (Indrehus and Vassbotn, 2001) tunnel NO$_\chi$ concentrations were as high as 1.0 ppm; therefore, people were exposed to extremely high NO$_x$.

In addition, to determine the actual impact of tunnel NO$_x$ on exposure levels, the contamination of cabin air in vehicles should be considered.

New air-conditioned cars are equipped with high-efficiency air conditioning systems that only utilize filter devices to remove particulate matter. Meanwhile, gas pollutants penetrate into the cabin, and thus, exposure rises to extremely high concentrations. Finally, exposure can be substantially increased in the case of peak-hour and unexpected (accident) traffic congestions (Barrefors, 1996). It is, therefore, obvious that specific measures should be taken to control and reduce air pollution levels even in short tunnels such as the suitable operation of ventilation systems and maintenance of automobiles to reduce emissions.

REFERENCES

Barrefors, G. Air pollution in road tunnels. *The Science of the Total Environment*. 1996;190:431-435.

Bellasio, R. Modeling air pollution in road tunnels. *Atmospheric Environment*. 1997; 21:1539-1551.

Chan, L. Y., Zeng, L., Qin, Y., Lee, S. C. CO concentration inside the cross-harbor tunnel in Hong-Kong. *Environment International*. 1996;22:405-409.

Chang, T. Y., Modzelewski, S. W., Norbeck, J. M., Pierson, W. R. Tunnel air quality and vehicle emissions. *Atmospheric Environment*. 1981;15:1011-1016.

De Fre, R., Bruynseraede, P., Kretzschmar, J. C. Air pollution measurements in traffic tunnels. *Environmental Health Perspectives*. 1994;102:31-37.

El-Fadel, M., Hashisho, Z. Vehicular emissions and air quality assessment in roadway tunnels: the Salim Slam tunnel. *Transportation Research Part D: Transport and Environment*. 2000;D5:355-372.

Fraser, M., Cass, G., Simoneit, B. R. T. Gas-phase and particle-phase organic compounds emitted from motor vehicle in a Los Angeles Roadway tunnel. *Environmental Science and Technology*. 1998;32:2051-2060.

Funasaka, K., Miyazaki, T., Kawaraya, T., Tsuruho, K., Mizuno, T. Characteristics of particulates and gaseous pollutants in a highway tunnel. *Environmental Pollution*. 1998;102:171-176.

Garshick, E., Laden, F., Hart, J. E., Rosner, B., Smith, T. J., Dockery, D. W., Spiezer, F. E. Lung cancer in railroad workers exposed to diesel exhaust. *Environmental Health Perspectives*. 2004;122:1539-1543.

Garshick, E., Schenker, M. B., Munoz, A., Segal, M., Smith, T. J., Woskie, S. R., Hammond, S. K., Speizer, F. E. A retrospective cohort study of lung cancer and diesel exhaust exposure in railroad workers. *American Review of Respiratory Disease*. 1988;137:820-825.

Gertler, A. W., Fujita, E. M., Pierson, W. R., Wittorf, D. N. Appointment of NMHC tailpipe vs non-tailpipe emissions in the Fort McHenry and Tuscarora Mountain Tunnels. *Atmospheric Environment*. 1996;30:2297-2305.

Gilbert, N. L., Woodhouse, S., Stied, D. M., Brook, J. R. Ambient nitrogen dioxide and distance from a major highway. *The Science of the Total Environment*. 2003;312:43-46.

Goldberg, M. S., Parent, M. E., Siemiatycki, J., Desy, M., Nadon, M., Richardson, L., Lakhani, R., Latreille, B., Valois, M. F. A case-control study of the relationship between the risk of colon cancer in men and exposures to occupational agents. *American Journal of Industrial Medicine*. 2001;39:531-546.

Indrehus, O., Vassbotn, P. CO and NO$_2$ pollution in a long two-way traffic road tunnel: investigation of NO$_2$/NO$_x$ ratio and modelling of NO$_2$ concentration. *Journal of Environmental Monitoring*. 2001;3:220-225.

Laden, F., Hart, J. E., Smith, T. J., Davis, M. E., Garshick, E. Cause-specific mortality in the unionized trucking industry. *Environmental Health Perspectives*. 2007;115:1192-1196.

McLaren, R., Gertler, A. W., Wittor, D. N., Belzer, W., Dann, T., Singleton, D. L. Real-world measurements of exhaust and evaporative emissions in the Cassiar Tunnel predicted by chemical mass balance. *Environmental Science and Technology*. 1996;30:3001-3009.

Pucher, K., Zwiener, K. Air quality inside a tunnel tube and in the vicinity of the tunnel portals. In: *Proceedings of the AWMA 90th annual meeting*. 1997;MP6.01, Toronto, Canada.

Riediker, M., Cascia, W. E., Griggs, T. R., Herbst, M. C., Bromberg, P. A., Neas, I., Williams, R. W., Devlin, R. B. Particulate matter exposure in cars is associated with cardiovascular effects in healthy young men. *American Journal of respiratory and Critical Care Medicine*. 2004;169:934-940.

Rogak, S. N., Pott, U., Dann, T., Wang, D., Gaseous emissions from vehicles in a traffic tunnel in Vancouver, BC. *Journal of the Air and Waste Management Association*. 1998;48:604-615.

Roorda-Knape, M. C., Janssen, N. A. H., de Hartog, J., Van Vliet, P. H. N., Harssema, H., Brunekreef, B. Traffic related air pollution in cities near motorways. *The Science of the Total Environment*. 1999;235:339-341.

Steenland, K., Deddens, J., Stayner, L. Diesel exhaust and lung cancer in the trucking industry: exposure-response analyses and risk assessment. *American Journal of Industrial Medicine*. 1998;34:220-228.

Suppan, P., Schadler, G. The impact of highway emissions on ozone and nitrogen oxide levels during specific meteorological conditions. *The Science of the Total Environment*. 2004;334-335:215-222.

World Road Organization. Pollution by nitrogen dioxide in road tunnels. PIARC Publ. 05.9.B. 2000.

Chapter 3

EVALUATION OF A SAFE PATIENT HANDLING PROGRAM AMONG HEALTH CARE WORKERS

Hyun J. Lim[1] and Timothy R. Black[2]
[1] College of Medicine, University of Saskatchewan, Canada
[2] Human Resources Division, University of Saskatchewan, Canada

ABSTRACT

The burden of musculoskeletal injuries (MSI) among patient handling health care workers is very high. Efforts to reduce work related MSI injuries have shown mixed results, and strong evidence for intervention effectiveness is lacking. The objectives of our study were (i) to evaluate the effectiveness of a multi-factor Transfer, Lifting and Repositioning (TLR) safe patient handling program among health care workers; and (ii) to evaluate the long-term effect based on repeated injury following this TLR intervention program. This study was a quasi-experimental study design, utilizing a non-randomized control group. Data were collected from six hospitals in Saskatchewan, Canada from September 1, 2001 to December 1, 2006. A total of 766 TLR injury cases were reported from 1480 eligible individuals for the study. Of the 1480 individuals, 149 (15.3%) in the control group and 114 (11.5%) in the intervention group experienced repeated MSI injuries during the study period. Analysis of all injury rates (medical aide and time-loss combined), time-loss only injury rates, rate ratios, and rate differences showed significant differences between the intervention and control groups. The study provides significant evidence for the effectiveness of a multi-factor TLR program for patient-handling health care workers, especially in small hospitals. Implementing a multi-factor program with the right equipment and training can lower the risk of injury among health care workers. The synergistic relationships between components of a multi-factor intervention and applicability of injury prevention programs to different settings, such as home care and critical care, need to be further explored.

INTRODUCTION

Patient handling injuries are common among health care workers, and the risk of injury increases with the number of patient handling tasks performed (Concha-Barrientos et al., 2004; U.S. Department of Labor, 2005). Among patient handling health care workers, the burden of musculoskeletal injuries (MSI) is very high and especially back pain is prevalent (Engkvist et al., 2000; Maul et al., 2003; Bejia et al., 2005; Bos et al., 2007; Landry et al., 2008). A comprehensive review of back pain prevalence studies in nursing personnel indicated a pattern of prevalence rates from 47% to 75% (Maul et al., 2003; Heap, 1987; Trinkoff et al., 2002; Tezel, 2005; Cunningham et al., 2006). Nursing personnel also have the highest back-related workers' compensation claim rates of any occupation and are among the highest at risk for musculoskeletal disorders (Bonauto et al., 2006). A high prevalence of MSI also contributes significantly to high patient care cost and to the shortage of nursing personnel (Concha-Barrientos et al., 2004; Bonauto et al., 2006).

In many studies dealing with the relationship between low back disorders and ergonomic work factors, evidence for an association of low back disorders with lifting was reported, and a positive dose-response relationship was found (NIOSH, 2007). The attributable fraction of disease burden due to occupational exposure to ergonomic stressors is estimated at 37% for the low back pain (Concha-Barrientos et al., 2004). Patient handling activities subject health workers to high biomechanical loads (Marras et al., 1999; Zhuang et al., 2000). If standard manual patient handling techniques continue to be used, possibly because they are more time efficient, then such techniques can be improved to reduce the biomechanical hazard (Nelson et al., 2003). Reducing the risk for MSI related to patient handling requires not only the reduction of biomechanical forces involved with each activity, but also the reduction of overall exposure to patient handling. Frequent lifting has been shown to be associated with earlier onset of back injury compared to infrequent lifting, irrespective of nursing occupation (Stobbe et al., 1988). Other tasks such as moving occupied beds, moving other heavy equipment, and holding patient limbs while applying anti-embolism stockings add to the biomechanical stresses experienced by nursing personnel (Waters et al., 2007). All manual transfer and repositioning techniques pose an increased risk based on spinal loading (Marras et al., 1999; Zhuang et al., 2000). Studies have suggested that the implementation of ceiling lifts may reduce musculoskeletal injuries and that they may prove cost effective through a reduction of injury claims (Zhuang et al., 1999; Ronald et al., 2002; Chhokar et al., 2005). Since an aging population has created the need for proactive injury prevention in health care workers and patients/residents have become heavier over time, facilities have purchased additional patient handling equipment and have implemented body mechanics training.

The transfer, lifting and repositioning (TLR) program under scrutiny in our study was intended to reduce MS injuries, in part, by defining, assessing and standardizing the patient handling (transfers, lifts and repositioning) requirements and procedures for each individual patient to ensure both patient and worker safety and implementing a training program which emphasized and reinforced minimizing physical effort through the maximum use of equipment. Many studies also suggest that education and training alone, without work modifications, does not decrease the number of occupational low back injuries (Videman et al., 1989; Garg, 1999; Johnsson et al., 2002; Edlich et al., 2005). Prior to implementation of the educational component, patient handling equipment was provided to bring all high needs units to the same equipment complement level.

A TLR program may prevent injuries incurred while performing one type of maneuver and not another, depending on the emphasis of the intervention. Also, some patient handling maneuvers may be more stressful, pose a higher risk of injury and thus have a greater potential for improvement. Ronald et al. found no significant change in overall MSI rates or repositioning MSI injury rates but did see a significant reduction in injury rates related to transferring and lifting injuries (Ronald, et al., 2002). The lack of improvement in overall MSI rates in the Ronald et al. study may have been due to the mild changes that their intervention made, that is, changes in mechanical lift type, the implementation of a new policy encouraging the use of transfer belts, and a "no manual lifting" policy (Ronald, et al., 2002). However, Collins et al. showed that post-intervention reductions were observed for injuries associated with unclassified transfers, bed to chair and chair to bed transfers and turning/rolling, toileting or lifting a patient off the floor, breaking a resident's fall and repositioning in bed (Collins et al., 2002). Garg et al. (2007) studied the long-term effect of "zero-lift program" adopting a participatory-team approach with modern, battery operated, portable hoists and other patient transfer assistive devices. Their studies showed improvements in patient comfort and safety and less soreness and tiredness at the end of their shifts among nursing personnel (Garg, 1999; Garg et al., 2007). The primary aims of our study were (i) to evaluate the effectiveness of a multi-factor TLR safe patient handling program among health care workers; and (ii) to evaluate the long-term effect based on repeated injury following this TLR intervention program. Evidence of effectiveness would also provide further justification for program cost. Although many studies suggest the effectiveness of multi-factor injury prevention interventions on reduction of MSIs among health care workers, little is known about the risk of repeated injury after a multi-factor TLR intervention program. Therefore, we also investigated the risk of repeated patient handling injuries following the implementation of a multi-factor injury prevention program. Positive results would provide an incentive for other hospitals to implement similar programs, if they have not done so already.

METHODOLOGY

This was a quasi-experimental study which involved a TLR intervention group and a non-randomized control group. This study was conducted in two Health Regions (6 hospitals) in Saskatchewan, Canada, from September 1, 2002 to December 1, 2006. The TLR program was implemented in the intervention group (3 hospitals: A, B, and C). Hospital A was a large, tertiary hospital having 436 beds. The intervention period for Hospital A was from September 2002 to June 2004. Hospital B was a medium sized community hospital having 239 beds. The intervention period for Hospital B was from September 2002 to September 2004. Hospital C was a small hospital with a long-term care facility having 240 residents. The intervention period for Hospital C was from January 2005 to December 2005. The control group (3 hospitals: D, E, and F) were matched to the intervention hospitals by hospital types (i.e., community hospital, long-term care, and tertiary care) and hospital size. The descriptors of the type of hospital, large tertiary care, community hospital and rehabilitation/long term care were based on the general types of services provided by the Occupational Health & Safety (OH&S) Department of each Health Region to determine comparability from an injury potential standpoint. For example, both of the hospitals classified as large had trauma centers where the risk of injury was considered high as well as large general medical and surgical wards. The small hospitals both had long term care and rehabilitation programs where the high risk of patient handling injuries is well known. The best measure of exposure to risk of injury available in this study was Full Time Equivalents (FTE). Hence, the hospitals were matched on hospital type and size based on FTEs. Table 1 provides the study hospital characteristics in detail.

Table 1. Characteristics of the Intervention and Control Group Hospitals

Group	Size	Type	Services provided	number of available beds
Intervention	Large (A)	Tertiary Care Hospital	Trauma, maternal and child services, neurosurgery, cardiovascular surgery, teaching	436 average over study period
	Medium (B)	Community Hospital	MRI suite, Breast Health Centre, Eye care centre, geriatric assessment, gynecology and rehabilitation units, Neuroscience research centre, general rehabilitation services, sleep disorders	239 average over study period
	Small (C)	Long-term Care Facility	Heavy and specialized care, geriatric Re-Enablement Unit, Emergency and planned respite, Long term and short stay, community day program	240 residents
Control	Large (D)	Acute Care Facility	Ambulatory care, cardiosciences, critical care, intensive care, diagnostic imaging, trauma and emergency services, mental health, renal dialysis, sleep disorders, women and children's health services	383 average over study period
	Medium (E)	Community Hospital	Orthopedics, ophthalmology, cancer care, ambulatory care, Critical care ICU, CCU, diagnostic imaging, emergency services, eye centre, palliative care, therapy services, surgical care, ostomy and wound clinic, dermatology clinic	216 average over study period
	Small (F)	Rehabilitation Centre	Functional Rehabilitation, Amputee Services, Spinal Cord Injury Services and Orthopedics, Children's Services, Adult Rehabilitation, Extended Care and Veteran's Services	306 average over the study period

Table 2. All injuries and FTE for one year pre-intervention period by study hospital type

Intervention Group Hospital size	# of all injuries/ FTE	Control Group Hospital size	# of all injuries/ FTE
Large (A)	104 / 1073	Large (D)	75 / 1166
Medium (B)	78 / 504	Medium (E)	48 / 488
Small (C)	78 /194	Small (F)	67 / 391
Total	260 / 1771	Total	190 / 2044

* FTE=full time equivalent; 1 FTE=1950 hours; per 100 FTE.

Table 2 provides the number of injuries (non-time loss and time loss) and FTE for one year pre-intervention period by the study hospital.

In our study, the TLR intervention consisted of an injury prevention program which utilized ergonomic principles. This included engineering and administrative controls. The TLR intervention program component consisted of staff education on anatomy, injuries, body mechanics, personal health, lifting and patient handling procedures, standardized patient handling needs assessment, warning signage (TLR placards) and patient handling algorithms (a decision making tree that standardized the criteria for selecting which patient handling method is required for each patient).

A "hands-on" patient-handling skills development component was included as part of the one-day educational sessions to allow for skills based learning in equipment usage and to provide feedback on patient-handling technique. Training began with an eight hour training session. A course booklet and training materials were given to the workers for their later reference. Participation in these training sessions was mandatory for all workers who regularly handled patients. There was also an ongoing TLR training, through the on-ward coaches. The follow up requirement for personnel was either one hour per year or four hours every three years. Patient handling equipment including total body lifts, sit-stand lifts, ceiling track lifts, slings, slider sheets, repositioning sheets, turning sheets and transfer belts was provided in the intervention group. The provision of this equipment preceded the educational component of the intervention and was considered part of the TLR program. In our study, all health workers required to regularly handle patients were eligible for the study. Other occupations such as housekeeping, maintenance, security, and administration were excluded. Injury cases were restricted to MSI only and defined as those that occurred during a patient handling maneuver. Injuries that occurred in patient handling staff that occurred during other material handling tasks were not included. Once an injury occurs in a musculoskeletal structure, subsequent risk of injury in that body part is increased, especially for spinal injuries. Thus, previous injuries, in the same body part, occurring in subjects within the study period were excluded for both the intervention and control hospitals. For repeated injuries, employee identifier numbers were used for the intervention group. For the control group, because each individual was not identified as a unique employee, date of birth, department worked, profession, body part injured, and/or the previous injury variable were used where available. Each intervention and control hospital were followed for two years after completion of the intervention program. Figure 1 shows the data extraction flowchart.

Our study used administrative data extracted from the OH&S Departments in the Health Regions to which the intervention and control hospitals belonged. The intervention group dataset was complete for variables: age, sex, length of service, classification of injuries by TLR cause, non-time-loss injuries, time-loss injuries, body part injured, type of maneuver causing injury (TLR injury), lost time days/injury, and claim cost/injury. The control group dataset was incomplete for age, sex, length of service, classification of injuries by TLR cause, time-loss days and claim cost. Data on time-loss and non-time loss injuries, lost time days, and claims costs were collected from both groups for corresponding one year pre- and one year post-intervention time periods. All injuries and all injuries rates were also analyzed. In our study, all injuries refer to both non-time loss and time loss injuries taken together. The inclusion criteria for both non-time loss and time loss injuries is all MSIs occurring during a patient handling maneuver in patient handling personnel. Time loss injuries were then analyzed separately, as these are of more concern and more cost to the organization. The other outcome was the event of TLR related "repeated" injury (yes/no) occurring in individuals within the study time.

Descriptive statistics were used to summarize the data. For continuous variables, a Student's t-test was used to compare the two groups. For categorical variables, a Chi-square test or Fisher's exact test was used to compare the groups. Outcome data (claim cost and time-loss days) were analyzed with non-parametric Mann-Whitney U test, as these data were not normally distributed. Injury rates were based on the number of injured workers in the numerator and the number of total hours worked for all TLR trained employees, or their counterparts in the control group, converted to full time equivalents (FTE) as the denominator. The denominator was standardized to FTEs, where one FTE = 1950 hours worked hours, to adjust for the differences in the exposure between and within groups. Univariate and multivariate Poisson regression models were performed for analysis of count data (Neter et al., 1996). For the repeated injury outcome, logistic regression models were performed. Interactions in the final model were checked. A 0.05 alpha level was used for statistical significance. All analyses in this study were performed using STATA statistical analysis software version 10.0 (Stata Corp LP, College Station, Texas) and SAS statistical software version 9.2 (The SAS Institute, Gary, NC). This project received operational and ethics approval from both Health Regions and the University of Saskatchewan.

RESULTS

A total of 2505 injuries were reported in the dataset. Of those, 1953 TLR related injuries from 1480 individuals were reported and eligible for the present study (n= 789 for the intervention group and n= 691 for the control group; Figure 1). Of the study population, 149 (15.3%) in the control group and 114 (11.5%) in the intervention group had repeated MSI injuries (Yes/No).

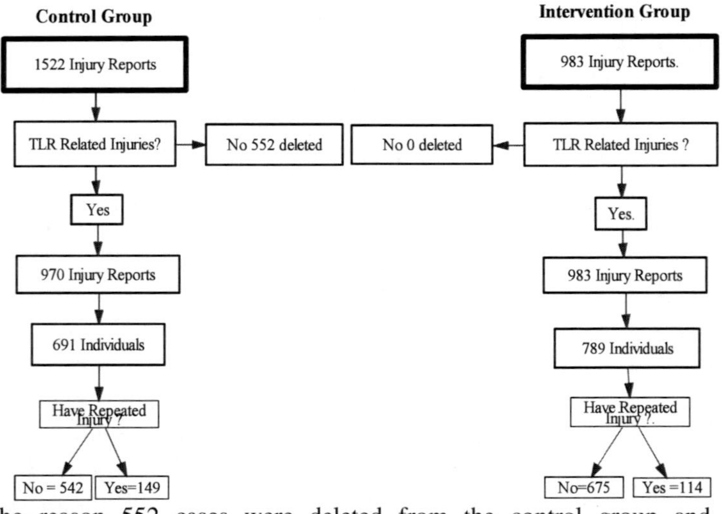

Note: The reason 552 cases were deleted from the control group and 0 from intervention group is due to fact that the control health region reported all injuries, not just TLR related injuries.

Figure 1. Data extraction flowchart.

Table 3. Baseline characteristics of the study subjects

Variables	Intervention (N=789)	Control (N=691)
Gender Female	734 (93%)	628 (91%)
Male	55 (7%)	63 (9%)
Age (mean ± s.d.)	41.2 ± 10.1	39.3 ± 10.2
Occupation		
Nursing RN *	451 (57%)	359 (52%)
LPN	105 (13%)	128 (18%)
RPN	0 (0%)	1 (0.2%)
Nurse Aides	12 (1.5%)	66 (9.5%)
Attendants	159 (20%)	33 (5%)
Clerks/Unit Assistants	28 (4%)	0 (0%)
Other **	34 (4%)	104 (15%)
Hospital		
Small	180 (23%)	241 (35%)
Medium	230 (29%)	187 (27%)
Large	379 (48%)	263 (38%)

* RN = registered nurses; LPN = *licensed practical nurses*; RPN = registered psychiatric nurse.

** Others include physical therapists, occupational therapists, recreational therapists, paramedic, unit supporter, operation room technician, etc.

The average age of the injured health care worker was approximately 40 years old and more than 90% of them were females. The majority were nurses. Table 3 shows the characteristics of the study subjects in detail.

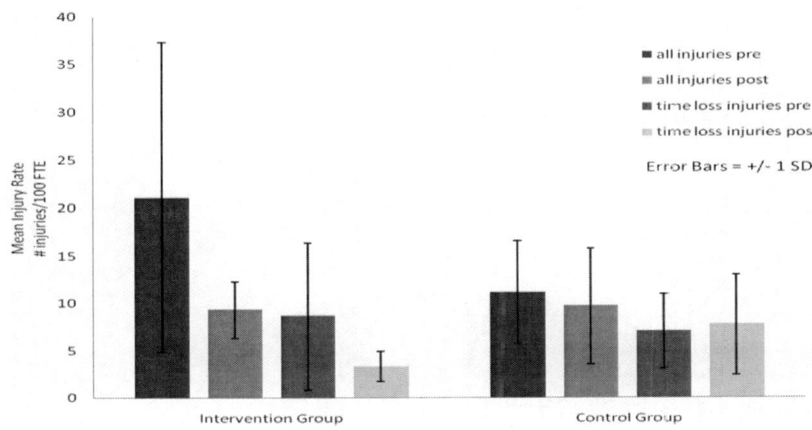

Figure 2. Mean Injury Rates.

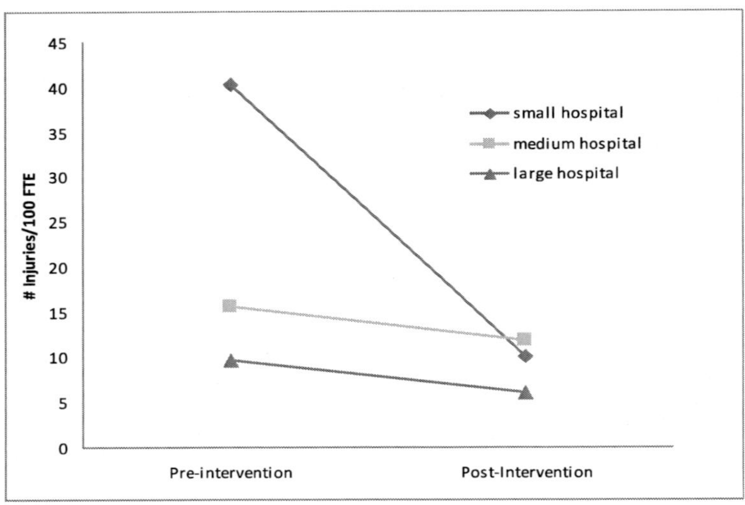

Figure 3. All injuries in intervention group by hospital size.

Our study results suggested that the intervention group had a significant improvement in injury rates and time loss injuries comparing to the control group (Figure 2). The intervention group decreased for all injuries (no time-loss and time-loss combined) but the control groups decreased to a lesser degree (Figures 3 & 4).

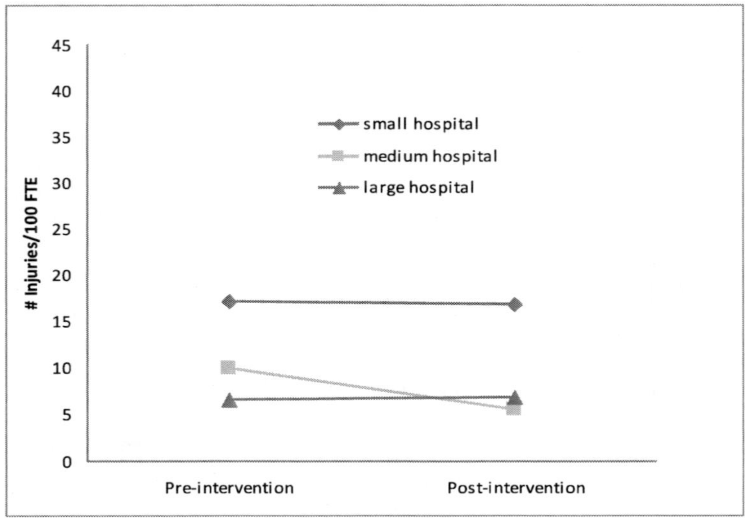

Figure 4. All injuries in control group by hospital size.

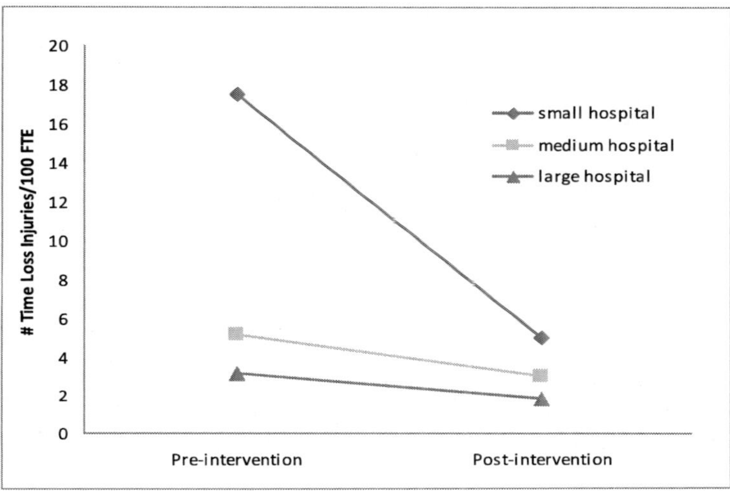

Figure 5. Time-loss injuries in intervention group by hospital size.

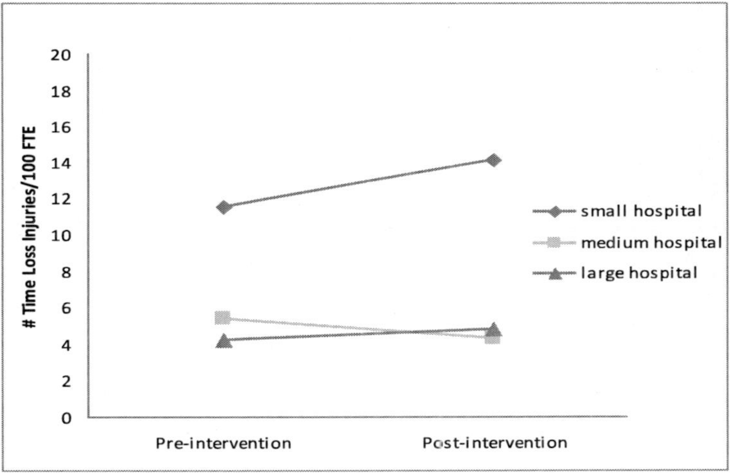

Figure 6. Time-loss injuries in control group by hospital size.

The analysis also revealed significant reductions for time-loss injuries in the intervention group in contrast to the non-significant changes in the control group (Figures 5 & 6). Within the intervention group, a significant reduction of all injuries in the small intervention hospital but less reduction in medium and large intervention hospitals was observed (Figures 3). Similarly, time-loss injuries showed different reduction for the different size hospitals within the intervention group (Figure 5).

Multivariate Poisson regression analysis also revealed similar reductions for all injury and time-loss injuries in the intervention group. All injuries rate ratios indicated that, controlling for hospital size, the relative rate of MSI for patient handling personnel was reduced by 30.7% in the intervention group post-intervention (RR=0.69; 95% CI= 0.6 - 0.8; p < 0.0001; Table 4-i). The positive rate ratio obtained for the group variable represented elevated risk of injury in the intervention group compared to the control group occurring both before and after the intervention for all injuries.

Poisson regression analysis also revealed similar reductions for time-loss injuries in the intervention group (RR=0.81, 95% CI=0.68-0.96, p-value=0.044; Table 4-ii). Here, the rate of time loss MSI for patient handling personnel was lower for the intervention group compared to the control group. No significant interaction between covariates was observed in the multivariate analysis.

Of the 1480 study population, 149 (15.3%) in the control group and 114 (11.5%) in the intervention group had repeated MSI injuries during the study period. Our data showed that regardless of hospital size, the intervention hospitals had consistently fewer repeated injuries than the control hospitals (Figure 7).

Table 4. Multivariate Poisson regression analysis of (i) all injuries and (ii) time-loss injuries with rate ratio and 95% confidence interval

	Covariate	Rate Ratio	95% CI	P-value
	Intervention period *	0.693	0.600 – 0.800	<0.0001
(i) all injuries	Group **	1.422	1.231 – 1.642	<0.0001
	Hospital size			
	small	1.00		
	medium	0.513	0.425 – 0.619	<0.0001
	large	0.346	0.292 – 0.411	<0.0001
(ii) time-loss	Intervention period *	0.814	0.667 - 0.995	0.044
injuries	Group **	0.721	0.585 - 0.889	0.002
	Hospital size			
	small	1.00		
	medium	0.384	0.294 - 0.501	<0.0001
	large	0.298	0.150 - 0.375	<0.0001

* Reference category is pre-intervention period.
** Reference category is the control group.

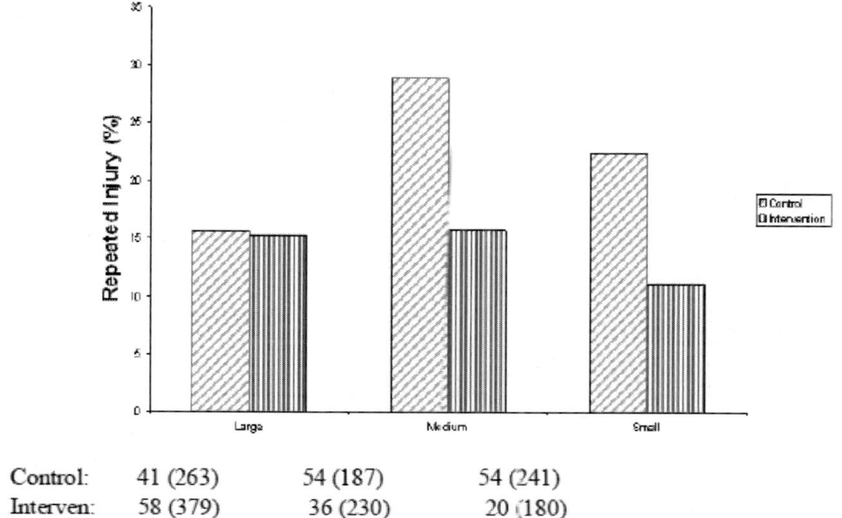

Control:	41 (263)	54 (187)	54 (241)
Interven:	58 (379)	36 (230)	20 (180)

* The number of repeated injuries and the individuals belonging to each category in parenthesis. Chi-square test (or **Fisher's** exact test) was used.

Figure 7. Proportion of repeated injury by hospital size.

The medium and small size hospitals in the intervention group had significantly fewer repeated injuries than in the control group (p-values =0.001 and 0.002, respectively). For each category of occupation, the intervention group also had consistently fewer repeated injuries than the control group (Figure 8). Registered nurses (RN)/general duty nurses (GDN), and Others (Therapists, Technicians, Unit Supporters, etc.) had significantly fewer repeated injuries in the intervention group than in the control group (p=0.016 and p=0.009, respectively).

Multivariate logistic regression analysis indicated that that the intervention group had a 38.1% lower odds of having repeated MSI injury compared to the control group, after adjusting for hospital size (OR=0.618; 95% CI= 0.27 - 0.81; p =0.0005). No statistically significant interaction emerged between hospital size and group.

In our study, claim cost/injury and time-loss days/injury both decreased after the TLR program in the intervention group (p-values = 0.09 & 0.013; Note that the data for the control group were not available). Mean claim cost/injury decreased from $3,891 to $2.302 (41% reduction) and mean time-loss days/claim decreased from 35.99 days to 16.2 days (55% reduction). The greatest improvement for both claim cost/injury and time-loss days/injury was made in the small hospital.

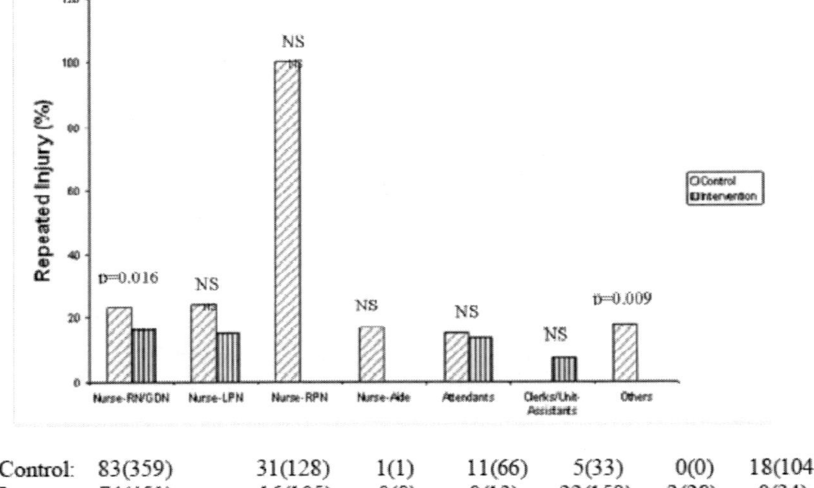

	Control:		Interven:
Control:	83(359)	31(128)	1(1)	11(66)	5(33)	0(0)	18(104)
Interven:	74(451)	16(105)	0(0)	0(12)	22(159)	2(28)	0(34)

* The number of repeated injuries and the individuals belonging to each category in parenthesis. Others include physical therapists, occupational therapists, recreational therapists, operation room technicians, dispatch porters, etc. Chi-square test (or Fisher's exact test) was used.

Figure 8. Proportion of repeated injury by occupation.

DISCUSSION

We examined the effectiveness of an administrative and engineering intervention for patient handling in three different types of hospitals. The study results showed that the use of a multi-factorial injury prevention program can significantly reduce all injuries, time-loss, and claim costs/injury, which represented a substantial benefit to the intervention hospitals. The study also showed that this intervention program sustained when we examined the risk of TLR related repeated injury. The effect of the intervention seemed to be greater in the small hospital than in the medium or large sized hospitals.

Our study found significant decreases in lifting injuries following implementation of the TLR intervention program. Some patient handling maneuvers may be more biomechanically stressful, pose a higher risk of injury and thus have a greater potential for improvement. A rigorous analysis of the maneuver type variable was not possible in this study due to the lack of control group data and the level at which the data was collected. However, our study was unique in its ability to examine the effectiveness of a multi-factor ergonomic intervention in relation to hospital size using a quasi-experimental design with injury rates, repeated injuries, time-loss days, and claims costs as outcome measures. It provides a more detailed comparison of the effect of an injury prevention intervention in health-care hospitals of different size and type. Our results are similar to other studies with roughly comparable interventions in terms of outcome measures, intervention applied, study population and setting (Collins et al., 2004; Lynch and Freunda, 2000; Nelson et al., 2006). The injury rate reductions in our study are similar in magnitude to Collins et al. (2004). Other studies showed that injury rate reduction was similar in direction, but not in magnitude, compared to our study (Nelson et al., 2006; Yassi et al., 2001; Evanoff et al., 2003; Li et al., 2004). Yassi et al. found no statistically significant change in injury rates comparing a control group with a three hour training intervention group in a large hospital (Yassi et al., 2001). Their result may have been due to a limited potential for improvement in a large facility or that their interventions were not sufficiently effective. Our results comparing all-injury and time-loss injury rate ratios for small, medium and large hospitals showed a similar trend. However, the effect seemed to be more effective in the small hospital than in the medium or large sized hospital. It is possible that the differential effect of the intervention may have been due to differences in how the intervention was received (buy-in) or applied, how it was delivered, or the level of management support for the intervention. It is also suspected that the small hospital received more patient lifting equipment per hospital bed than the larger hospitals. To explain the apparent increase in intervention effect at the small hospital we must consider that the exposure to lifting tasks per FTE is likely to be higher at the small hospital than at the other hospitals due to the nature of the patient population. Thus, there may have been more potential for improvement when compared to the other hospitals. We were not able to determine exposure to patient lifting tasks for individual workers, and thus, we cannot differentiate this effect from other possible explanations.

In our study, like other published studies overall, mean time-loss days per claim decreased significantly (Collins et al., 2004; Lynch and Freunda, 2000; Nelson et al., 2006; Yassi et al., 2001, Hartvigsen et al., 2005). Number of time-loss days/injury including days on modified duty gives a measure of the duration of disability resulting from patient handling injuries and better represents any preventative effects of the intervention than overall time-loss days or time-loss days/FTE. The observed trend overall is that ergonomic interventions can produce significant reductions in total time-loss days and time-loss days/'injury which is supported by our study.

Our study revealed overall reductions in WCB claim costs/injury of 47.7% from the pre-to post-intervention periods. However, our study did not calculate claim cost/FTE, and thus, it is difficult to compare these results with others using this outcome measure. In our study, the reduction of claim costs observed in the intervention group showed a significant benefit, but it is not possible to attribute this reduction to the effect of the intervention without control group data. Where the outcome measures were similar, our results were similar to many other studies (Ronald et al., 2002; Collins et al., 2004; Lynch and Freunda, 2000; Li et al., 2004; Smedley et al., 2003). The significant reduction of time-loss days but not claim cost/injury may be a result of rising costs for medical treatment between the pre- and post-time periods. Medical costs per claim for individual injured workers, as reported by the Saskatchewan Workers' Compensation Board, have been steadily rising primarily due to rising costs for medical treatment (Workers' Compensation Board of Saskatchewan, 2007).

The burden of patient handling injuries among health care personnel is substantial, pervasive and costly, especially since nursing staff shortages lead to an increase in workload for other nurses or patient handling personnel and high patient care costs. A multi-factor TLR intervention program may help to retain experienced health care workers and enhance workplace accommodations for permanently injured workers or workers returning to work from injury (Collins et al., 2004; Shamian et al., 2003; Cohen, 2006). Economic analyses have demonstrated that the initial investment in lifting equipment and employee training can be recovered in less than three years through reduction in workers' compensation expenses (Garg, 1999; Collins et al., 2004; Nelson et al., 2006; Tiesman et al., 2003). In a study of injury trends spanning 3 years pre-intervention and 3 years post-intervention, Chhokar et al. (2005) found that using a ceiling mounted device resulted in a significant and sustained decrease in lost work days and workers' compensation claims, which are considered direct costs associated with patient handling injuries. However, their study did not include a control group, which makes it difficult to ascertain the direct influence of the ceiling lifting devices on reducing injury claim rates and costs.

Our study has several limitations. Because we used administrative data in this study, the quality of data set was a concern. The study was weakened by the lack of information on the subject's detailed demographic and injury characteristics and the total number of employees at the site. The short study follow-up time might not be enough to reach a definite conclusion on the durability of the intervention effect. This measurement time span was also not long enough to capture fully matured WCB claims information (lost time days and claim costs), and thus, these measures may be underestimated. However, data collection time frames for similar size hospitals were identical in the control and intervention group. This helped to reduce the influence of selection-history threat as events would be occurring simultaneously in both groups. The addition of FTE data for each worker would have allowed for calculation of person-time denominators and a more exact determination of exposure and control of drop-outs, new worker influx and migration of workers between worksites or departments within a hospital. Injury rates were calculated based on FTEs, and this takes into account the change in exposure for the at-risk group of workers. A variety of outcome measures used in our study, such as all injuries, time-loss injuries, lost time days/injury and claim cost/injury, are not perhaps the most sensitive, compared to symptom reports, but they are not subject to biases resulting from the use of symptom report questionnaires (recall bias, validity and reliability issues with the instrument, obsequiousness bias, and/or poor response rate). Prior research has shown a previous history of back pain has shown to be a risk for future episodes of back pain (Videman et al., 1989; Lagerstrom et al., 1998), but in our study, patient's injury history was not available. Thus, a full regression analysis with such covariates, collected at the level of the worker and included in the analysis, could not be made.

CONCLUSION

The study provides significant evidence for the effectiveness of a multi-factor TLR program for patient-handling health care workers. Our results are especially relevant to smaller facilities, and this provides further strong impetus for implementation of this type of program where patient handling injury rates are high. Our study was unique in that it examined the effect of a TLR intervention in different size and type hospitals. Our findings suggested that different components of multi-factor intervention programs might needed for different hospital types. A possible future study would be aimed at tracking changes in injury rates and extending the post-intervention follow-up period to examine long-term sustainability of the intervention program. If injury rates remain reduced, this would add to the evidence for sustainability. If not, then this may indicate the need for subsequent retraining and reinforcement of the program. The baseline injury rate data could also be expanded with adequate resources. This would help clarify any pre-existing trends in injury rates that would provide an alternative explanation for the changes seen in this study. While there are many studies on patient handling injuries in health care workers, gaps still remain. Particularly, patient handling and MSIs in home care and critical care have not been sufficiently addressed. Implementing a multi-factor program with the right equipment and training can lower the risk of injury among health care workers. The synergistic relationships between components of multi-factor intervention programs and applicability of injury prevention programs to different healthcare settings, such as home care and critical care, need to be further explored.

ACKNOWLEDGMENTS

The authors wish to acknowledge the Saskatoon Health Region and the Regina Qu'Appelle Health Region for their support of this project.

REFERENCES

Bejia, I., Younes, M., Jamila, H. B., Khalfallah, T., Salem, K. B., Touzi, M., Akrout, M., Bergaoui, N. (2005). Prevalence and factors associated to low back pain among hospital staff. *Joint Bone Spine*, 72, 254-259.

Bonauto, D., Silverstein, B., Adams, D. (2006). Prioritizing industries for occupational injury and illness prevention and research, Washington state workers' compensation claims, 1999-2003. *Journal of Occupational and Environmental Medicine*, 48, 840-851.

Bos, E., Krol, B., van der Star, L., Groothoff, J. (2007). Risk factors and musculoskeletal complaints in non-specialized nurses, IC nurses, operation room nurses, and X-ray technologists. *International Archives of Occupational and Environmental Health*, 80, 198-206.

Chhokar, R., Engst, C., Miller, A., Robinson, D., Tate, R. B., Yassi, A. (2005). The three-year economic benefits of a ceiling lift intervention aimed to reduce healthcare worker injuries. *Applied Ergonomics*, 36, 223-229.

Cohen, J. D. (2006). The aging nursing workforce: how to retain experienced nurses. Journal of Healthcare Management, 51, 233-45.

Collins, J. W., Wolf, L., Bell, J., Evanoff, B. (2004). An evaluation of a "best practices" musculoskeletal injury prevention program in nursing homes. *Injury Prevention*, 10, 206-211.

Concha-Barrientos, M., Driscoll, T., Steenland, N., Punnett, L., Fingerhut, M., Prüss-Ustün, A., Corvalan, C., Leigh, J., Punnett, L., Tak, S. (2004). Selected occupational risk factors. In: Ezzati M, Lopez A, Rodgers A, Murray C editors. *Comparative quantification of health risks: global and regional burden of disease attributable to selected major risk factors.* World Health Organization, Geneva, pp. 1651-1802.

Cunningham, C., Flynn, T., Blake, C. (3006). Low back pain and occupation among Irish health service workers. *Occupational Medicine-Oxford,* 56, 447-454.

Edlich, R. F., Hudson, M. A., Buschbacher, R. M., Winters, K. L., Britt, L. D., Cox, M. J., Becker, D. G., McLaughlin, J. K., Gubler, K. D,. Zomerschoe, T. S., Latimer, M. F., Zura, R. D., Paulsen, N. S., Long, W. B. 3rd, Brodie, B. M., Berenson, S., Langenburg, S. E., Borel, L., Jenson, D. B., Chang, D. E., Chitwood, W. R. Jr, Roberts, T. H., Martin, M. J., Miller, A., Werner, C. L., Taylor, P. T. Jr, Lancaster, J., Kurian, M. S., Falwell, J. L. Jr, Falwell, R. J. (2005). Devastating injuries in healthcare workers: description of the crisis and legislative solution to the epidemic of back injury from patient lifting. *Journal of Long-Term Effects of Medical Implants,* 15, 225-241.

Engkvist, I. L., Hjelm, E. W., Hagberg, M., Menckel, E., Ekenvall, L. (2000). Risk indicators for reported over-exertion back injuries among female nursing personnel. *Epidemiology* 11, 519-522.

Evanoff, B., Wolf, L., Aton, E., Canos, J., Collins, J. (2003). Reduction in injury rates in nursing personnel through introduction of mechanical lifts in the workplace. *American Journal of Industrial Medicine,* 44, 451-457.

Garg, A. (1999). *Long-term effectiveness of "Zerolift program" in seven nursing homes and one hospital.* Cincinnati, Ohio: NIOSH. Contract No. U60/CCU512089-02.

Garg, A., Milholland, S., Deckow-Schaefer, G., Kapellusch, J. M. (2007). Justification for a minimal lift program in critical care. *Critical Care Nursing Clinics of North America,* 19, 187-196.

Hartvigsen, J., Lauritzen, S., Lings, S., Lauritzen, T. (2005). Intensive education combined with low tech ergonomic intervention does not prevent low back pain in nurses. *Occupational and Environmental Medicine,* 62, 13-17.

Heap, D. C. (1987). Low-back injuries in nursing staff. *Journal of the Society of Occupational Medicine* 37, 66-59.

Johnsson, C., Carlsson, R., Lagerstrom, M. (2002). Evaluation of training in patient handling and moving skills among hospital and home care personnel. *Ergonomics,* 45, 850-865.

Lagerstrom, M., Hansson, T., Hagberg, M. (1998). Work-related low-back problems in nursing. *Scandinavian Journal of Work, Environment and Health,* 24, 449-464.

Landry, M. D., Raman, S. R., Sulway, C., Golightly, Y. M., Hamdan, E. (2008). Prevalence and risk factors associated with low back pain among health care providers in a Kuwait hospital. *Spine* 33, 539-545.

Li, J., Wolf, L., Evanoff, B. (2004). Use of mechanical patient lifts decreased musculoskeletal symptoms and injuries among health care workers. *Injury Prevention,* 10, 212-216.

Lynch, R. M., Freunda, A. (2000). Short-term efficacy of back injury intervention project for patient care providers at one hospital. *American Industrial Hygiene Association Journal,* 61, 290-294.

Marras, W. S., Davis, K. G., Kirking, B. C., Bertsche, P. K. (1999). A comprehensive analysis of low-back disorder risk and spinal loading during the transferring and repositioning of patients using different techniques. *Ergonomics,* 42, 904-926.

Maul, I., Laubli, T., Klipstein, A., Krueger, H. (2003). Course of low back pain among nurses: a longitudinal study across eight years. *Occupational and Environmental Medicine,* 60, 497-503.

Nelson, A., Lloyd, J. D., Menzel, N., Gross, C. (2003). *Preventing nursing back injuries: redesigning patient handling tasks.* American Association of Occupational Health Nurses J, 51, 126-134.

Nelson, A., Matz, M., Chen, F. F., Siddharthan, K., Lloyd, J., Fragala, G. (2006). Development and evaluation of a multifaceted ergonomics program to prevent injuries associated with patient handling tasks. *International Journal of Nursing Studies,* 43, 717-733.

Neter, J., Kutner, M., Nachtsheim, C. (1996). *Applied Linear Statistical Models.* The McGraw-Hill Companies, New York.

NIOSH (National Institute for Occupational Safety and Health). 2007. Musculoskeletal Disorders and Workplace Factors: *A critical review of epidemiologic evidence for work-related musculoskeletal disorders of the neck, upper extremities and low back.* Edited by Bruce P. Bernard. DHHS (NIOSH) publication number 97-141.

Ronald, L. A., Yassi, A., Spiegel, J., Tate, R. B., Tait, D., Mozel, M. R. (2002). Effectiveness of installing overhead ceiling lifts. Reducing musculoskeletal injuries in an extended care hospital unit. *American Association of Occupational Health Nurses J.*, 50, 120-127.

Shamian, J., O'Brien-Pallas, L., Thomson, D., Alksnis, C., Kerr, M. S. (2003). Nurse Absenteeism, Stress and Workplace Injury: What are the contributing factors and what can/should be done about it? *International Journal of Sociology and Social Policy,* 23, 81-103.

Smedley, J., Trevelyan, F., Inskip, H., Buckle, P., Cooper, C., Coggon, D. (2003). Impact of ergonomic intervention on back pain among nurses. *Scandinavian Journal of Work Environment & Health*, 29, 117-123.

Stobbe, T. J., Plummer, R. W., Jensen, R. C., Attfield, M. D. (1988). Incidence of low-back injuries among nursing personnel as a function of patient lifting frequency. *Journal of Safety Research*, 19, 21-28.

Tezel A. Musculoskeletal complaints among a group of Turkish nurses. (2005). *International Journal of Neuroscience*, 115, 871-880.

Tiesman, H. M., Nelson, A., Charney, W., Siddharthan, K., Fragala, G. (2003). Effectiveness of a ceiling-mounted patient lift system in reducing occupational injuries in long term care. *Journal of Healthcare Safety*, 1, 34-40.

Trinkoff, A. M., Lipscomb, J. A., Geiger-Brown, J., Brady, B. (2002). Musculoskeletal problems of the neck, shoulder, and back and functional consequences in nurses. *American Journal of Industrial Medicine* 41, 170-178.

U.S. Department of Labor. (2005). *"Survey of occupational injuries & illnesses, summary estimates charts package"*. Bureau of Labor Statistics; Washington, DC: U.S. Department of Labor, Bureau of Labor Statistics, Safety and Health Statistics Program. http://www.bls.gov/iif/oshwc/osh/os/osch0032.pdf.

Videman, .T, Rauhala, H., Asp, S., Lindstrom, K., Cedercreutz, G., Kamppi, M., Tola, S., Troup, J. D. G. (1989). Patient-handling skill, back injuries, and back pain – an intervention study in nursing. *Spine,* 14, 148-156.

Waters, T. R., Nelson, A., Proctor, C. (2007). Patient handling tasks with high risk for musculoskeletal disorders in critical care. *Critical Care Nursing Clinics of North America*, 19, 131-143.

Workers' Compensation Board of Saskatchewan. (2007). *Annual Report* 2007. Regina, Saskatchewan, Canada. http://www.finance.gov.sk.ca/pacts /paccts08/compendium/reports/oe-Workers'%20Compensation% 20Board%20(Saskatchewan).pdf.

Yassi, A., Cooper, J. E., Tate, R. B., Gerlach, S., Muir, M., Trottier, J., Massey K. (2001). A randomized controlled trial to prevent patient lift and transfer injuries of health care workers. *Spine*, 26, 1739-1746.

Zhuang, Z. Q., Stobbe, T. J., Collins, J. W., Hsiao, H. W., Hobbs, G. R. (2000). Psychophysical assessment of assistive devices for transferring patients/residents. *Applied Ergonomics*, 31, 35-44.

Zhuang, Z. Q., Stobbe, T. J., Hsiao, H. W., Collins, J. W., Hobbs, G. R. (1999). Biomechanical *evaluation of assistive device for tranferring residents. Applied* Ergonomics, 30, 285-94.

In: Occupational Safety and Health
Editors: I.G. Kavouras, M.C.G. Chalbot © 2014 Nova Science Publishers, Inc.

ISBN: 978-1-63117-695-1

Chapter 4

EDUCATING IN OCCUPATIONAL SAFETY AND HEALTH: SCHOOLS AS CHANGE AGENTS

***Belén Gutiérrez-Villar, Rafael Araque-Padilla
and Maria José Montero-Simó***
Universidad Loyola Andalucía, Spain

ABSTRACT

There is an unquestionable social concern nowadays for the high number of work accidents worldwide. In spite of all the progress made, structural and individual factors still contribute to this problem. And without any doubt, part of the solution can be found in education, starting from its basic levels.

As a consequence, and in order to contribute to preventive as well as effective cultural practices, it is necessary that schools promote training in safe working practices and raise awareness of the main risk and danger factors. This can be accomplished in two ways: Students should be made aware of work related accident prevention and instilled with the principles of occupational safety and health, and staff (teaching and non-teaching) should be trained concerning the importance and necessity of occupational safety and health as a means to improve working conditions, as a basic principle and for educational value. The efficacy of the role of education in prevention revolves two practices: on one hand, the extent to which schools strengthen their commitment to teaching prevention and, on the other, the engagement of public institutions in its promotion. In this study, both perspectives are dealt with within the context of education in Andalusia (Spain). More particularly, the following two objectives were defined: to assess prevention within a broad set of educational values at Andalusian schools and to evaluate two of the primary awareness raising campaigns launched by the Regional Government of Andalusia at schools: Prevebús Joven and Aprende a Crecer con Seguridad. The methodology is based on a questionnaire sent to all Andalusian primary and secondary schools (2523) which generated a 28% response rate. The questionnaire was addressed to the Head of Studies of each of these schools, as directly responsible for the education at those levels. Besides, an institutional, rather than an individual perspective, was targeted. After a statistical analysis of the data, the results corresponding to the two objectives were evaluated. In relation to prevention culture and practice at Andalusian schools, the predisposition towards prevention, the measures already introduced, and their reasons and motivations will be discussed. Regarding the assessment of both public campaigns, an evaluation of the impact on the students as perceived by the school, both from a cognitive as well as a behavioral point of view, will be presented.

INTRODUCTION

The term Occupational Safety and Health (OSH) commonly refers to those measures taken in order to protect the health and safety of agents involved in any work environment and that aim to develop preventive behavior and attitudes during daily activities. One of these measures is "Education and Training for Prevention since childhood". Due to its impact on such relevant aspects as accidents, this concept guarantees and safeguards something as essential as life itself. We understand that schools should take measures in order to start building a culture of prevention and thus raise awareness of occupational risks and how to prevent them.

As a consequence, when talking about educating in OSH at schools, we consider that knowledge, which includes occupational risk prevention as well as a broader prevention culture, must be present within an educational context. We see education as the driving force in a society that we wish safe and healthy in both personal and professional behavior and attitudes. Following Hundeloh and Hess (2003), the sooner children, adolescents, and teachers become familiar with such concepts as safety and health, the faster they will develop risk awareness and thus shape their own personal and professional environment in a successful way.

It is worth questioning if our schools really work as effective change agents, how they see this task, their motivations and the difficulties they face, as well as the support provided by the public institutions. Consequently, the goal of this research is to provide knowledge as well as an assessment of primary and secondary schools as change agents. This study has been limited to the region of Andalusia (Southern Spain), but, although the situation in Andalusia might be different from other parts of Spain, it is our belief that this paper can offer valuable insights and be reproduced in other countries.

OCCUPATIONAL SAFETY AND HEALTH EDUCATION IN SCHOOLS WITHIN THE EU CONTEXT

Strategic Referents

Promoting a culture of prevention in schools is a relatively new concept within the European context. The joint Spanish EU Presidency and European Agency for Safety and Health at Work Seminar, organized in March of 2002 in cooperation with the European Commission, was considered to be the first step towards the integration of OSH into the European Union policies and practices regarding education.

The conference "Mainstreaming OSH into Education: the workers of tomorrow", organized in Rome in 2003 during the Italian Presidency, also played a relevant role in this effort by becoming the first stage of the model for European policies about OSH and education. The Rome declaration emphasizes the need for qualified and quantified goals in order to prepare children and adolescents for their working lives. It urges joint action by all involved parties, such as the European Economic and Social Committee, member states and social agents, in order to deal with this matter.

But, the most remarkable achievement is the recognition given to education by the Commission in the document: Adapting to change in work and society: a new Community strategy on health and safety at work 2002-2006. Here, the European Union strategy regarding safety and health for this period of time, explicitly points out education and training as key factors in the reinforcement of a culture of prevention. It argues that health and safety education does not begin at the workplace; it should be part of school curricula, either through awareness-rising activities, as a cross-cutting theme or transversal topic, or like a subject in its own right.

Some Occupational Safety and Health Education Experiences

The European Agency for Safety and Health at Work began its project "Mainstreaming Occupational Safety and Health into education in 2002" with the slogan: "start young, stay safe." The underlying concept was that the sooner children start to become familiar with concepts such as safety and health, the sooner they will be able to develop risk awareness and the better they can create their own safe and healthy environment for their future working and private lives.

Examples of good practice all over Europe and from different educational levels, primary, secondary and vocational education, were compiled in this study. The results of the analysis are shown in the report "Mainstreaming occupational safety and health into education. Good practice in school and vocational education." Here, the cases under study are classified into three groups, according to three different approaches:

- From a holistic approach, the case studies lend understanding in safety and health from a comprehensive point of view, which includes mental, physical and social well-being. They cover the whole educational system, focusing on a "school culture", as well as on the learning and working environments of students and teachers, respectively. There are 10 case studies from 6 countries, none of which were from the Spanish educational system.
- Those cases where safety and health are part of the curricula and OSH are not limited to one specific subject but integrated as transversal topics corresponding to a curricular approach. In other words, safety and health at work are present throughout all levels of education and as part of different subjects, as for example, foreign languages and literature. Also, here, the 10 projects are analyzed from four member states, three of them from Spain.
- From a workplace approach, the case studies deal with the transition from school to working life, the last and most important step of the educational process. Some of the examples focus on the students' introduction into the workplace, their path to professional lives and the risks they will have to face, either from a general level or

according to a specific sector. This is the group where almost 50% of the case studies reside (actually, 19), and they correspond to projects from 9 different European countries, none of them from Spain.

OCCUPATIONAL SAFETY AND HEALTH EDUCATION IN SCHOOLS IN SOUTHERN SPAIN (ANDALUSIA)

Strategic Referents

In recent years, the need to integrate prevention into the educational system has been promoted on a national level through institutional policies and actions, such as the creation of the Spanish Strategy on Safety and Health at Work for the period 2007-2012, in which objective 6.1. reads: "integrate safety and health into the curricula since elementary school as this would fight against social and educational exclusion."

Within the regional Andalusian context, the Governing Council of la Junta de Andalucía (Regional Government of Andalusia), following a proposal from the Regional Ministry of Education, approved the I Andalusian Plan for Occupational Health and Risk Prevention (2006-2010) for teachers at state schools, as a means for planning and coordinating all the activities carried out by state educational institutions in Andalusia regarding safety and health. The aim was to introduce a culture of prevention and promote quality management by integrating prevention into all the decisions, activities and administrative levels of these institutions.

We must also highlight Order 328/2010 of the 13th July 2010, which approves the Organic Law of infant and primary education (Section c: Risk Prevention and Safety and Health Promotion as Social and Cultural Assets, of Article 29: Fulfilment of Duties and Exercise of Right). Also, the Order of the 16th April 2008 regulates the procedure for the elaboration, approval and registry of a "Safety Plan" in all state schools in Andalusia. Besides, both the order and the safety plan informs risk prevention and safety and health promotion, as part of the School Regulations Plan. They integrate these aspects into the school as part of classroom organization and management as well as serve as a factor in influencing the quality of teaching.

Together with the initiatives above, where the need to transform schools into safe environments for the educational community is prioritized, what bears the closest relation to the present study are the General Plans for

Occupational Risks Prevention in Andalusia. In particular, the strategic objectives of the I General Plan for Occupational Risk Prevention (2003-2008) already included the introduction of a culture of prevention in Andalusian society. On the 31st December, 2008, this plan was finished and from several points of view became a milestone by providing the basis for the new planning framework for the period 2010-2014: Andalusian Strategy on Safety and Health at Work for the period 2010-2014. A strategy which presents, even in greater depth, those objectives which motivated this paper: to promote a culture of prevention:

a. Emphasizing social awareness of occupational risk prevention and reinforcing values and habits related to prevention in society.
b. Fostering and addressing occupational risk prevention at all educational levels (primary, secondary and vocational education).

Undertaken Initiatives

Several initiatives have been launched in Andalusia addressed to a young audience as a means to create a culture of prevention which can result in the strengthening of occupational safety and health. These initiatives do not expect short term outcomes, but a mid and long term sociological change. The activities developed can be grouped and summarized as follows:

A) Development and integration of educational modules into the curricula as transversal topics appropriate to each educational level. For example, the programme, Aprende a Crecer con Seguridad, introduces the culture of prevention in schools.

This project has four lines of action: teacher training; supporting guides in order to introduce this theme as a cross-cutting or transversal topic; studies on child accidents and other children's problems (like colour-blindness), and an awareness raising campaign at schools. The awareness raising campaign is carried out by a mobile unit, a mobile classroom bus which seats 24 students and is equipped with computers and audiovisual material.

This classroom-bus visits primary and secondary schools and addresses all the educational community, although its main target are students between the ages 10 and 12.

Chart 1. Advertising Material for the Campaign "Aprende a Crecer con Seguridad".

Chart 2. Advertising Material for the Campaign "Prevebús Joven".

The didactic material is designed around the character, Segurito (the campaign mascot), and includes informational material on different media types and audiovisual games. All of the materials have been created and developed by the staff from the Occupational Risks Prevention Schools at the provincial Delegations of the Regional Ministry of Employment. Twenty thousand students from 380 different towns and 427 schools have taken part in this program in Andalusia since 2004.

The main targets of this campaign are: a) to raise accident awareness among children, parents and teachers by promoting what the Occupational Risk Prevention Law calls a "culture of prevention;" b) to integrate parents, teachers and government agencies into this culture as active and influential elements on children's educational process; c) to reduce child accidents, and as a consequence, future occupational accidents and diseases, that is to say, child safety as a previous step towards occupational safety.

B) The program, Prevebús Joven, is a mobile classroom bus intended for providing information, raising awareness and training. Its target is to promote prevention as a value as well as to identify risks and avoid or control them by habit formation. It is carried out at Secondary Schools in Andalusia and includes one hour long interactive workshops addressed to students aged 14 to 16 and also informational sessions for teachers and parents on occupational risk prevention. In the first phase (2005-2006), Prevebús Joven visited 80 schools, 5,313 students attended the different activities, and 251 teachers and parents took part in the 468 informational sessions and workshops. In the second phase (2006-2007), 78 schools were visited, 6,303 students attended and 426 sessions and workshops were held.

AIMS OF THE INVESTIGATION

Based on the general aim of analyzing primary and secondary schools as change agents for the building of a better culture of prevention among adolescents, the following objectives have been specified:

- To analyze the schools' own initiatives towards a more proactive fulfilment of their role in promoting a culture of prevention. This means studying the schools' predisposition and motivation as well as the specific actions carried out.
- To evaluate the initiatives undertaken by the public institutions in order to promote prevention culture at schools. In particular, to attempt an evaluation of the campaigns: Aprende a Crecer con Seguridad and Prevebús Joven in two ways: 1) the impact of these awareness campaigns according to the Head of Studies' opinions on both cognitive and volitional levels and in the mid and long terms, not the short term. 2) The impact of the materials of Aprende a Crecer regarding their level of knowledge and availability
- To identify significant differences among the schools with respect to the culture of prevention, according to whether they took part in the campaigns Aprende a Crecer and/or Prevebús Joven or not, and whether the school was privately or publicly run.

In order to conduct the investigation, we took as starting points the main studies on the role of schools in the prevention of occupational risks conducted in Andalusia up to the present. In particular, there are two cases of special significance: Elementos didácticos y organizativos de la enseñanza de la prevención en el aula (2008), which includes a teacher questionnaire, and the final report of Valoración de la Campaña Aprende a Crecer (2009).

Both studies approach the real situation of schools regarding occupational risks prevention from different and complementary perspectives, and it is within this context that this study attempted to contribute with additional knowledge derived from the following differentiating characteristics:

- It took into account not the school faculty's but of the Head of Studies' opinions, as directly responsible for education at these levels. In this manner, we pursued the institutional perspective within the school regarding policy implementation and specific actions development.
- We approached the evaluation of the awareness campaigns launched by public institutions by searching for medium and long term impact and not for their immediate effects.
- The effectiveness of the complementary materials provided by the public institutions (guides, studies and advertising material) was analyzed regarding knowledge and availability. The content was not assessed from a pedagogical point of view.
- On the contrary, our study would have rather gone more deeply into the motivating and inhibiting aspects and into the predisposition and stance of schools as change agents.
- We searched for differences in prevention culture at schools, according to whether they are privately or publicly run and whether or not reached by public initiatives.

METHODOLOGY

Sample

In this study, a sample was chosen as relevant information units for our research, considering the size of our subject of analysis (2,523 schools in Andalusia) and its homogeneity. In particular, a simple random sampling was collected from an available schools directory.

The sample was stratified according to whether the school was visited by any of the two public campaigns (Prevebús Joven and Aprende a Crecer), trying to make the number of visited schools similar in relative terms to the general situation (approximately 10%).

Under these conditions, and in order to reach a level of confidence of 95%, the original design estimated a margin of error of 2.4% in the results for the whole region of Andalusia from a sample made up of 1000 units.

However, once collection tasks had begun and due to the low response rate obtained, it was decided to proceed with the sending the questionnaires to the whole population, as it became evident that the goal of 1000 responses could not be achieved by means of the original method. The sample eventually resulted in a census, which provided us with a total of 704 educational schools, which resulted in an error of 3.5% and a level of confidence of 95%.

Next, a short description of the profile of the final sample obtained was presented: 87.5% of the participating schools were publicly run and 12.5% of were private. Besides, considering their geographic location, most of them belong to the provinces of Cadiz (20.3%), Seville (19.6%) and Cordova (17.7%). Most of the schools we obtained information from provide primary education (almost 70%), followed by schools up to compulsory secondary education (24%) and, far in the third place, those which also provide noncompulsory secondary education (7.3%).

The imbalance in composition is consistent, at least from a qualitative point of view, with the real differences in the number of existing schools of each type in the whole population under study. 16.7% of all the surveyed schools were visited by one or both campaigns launched by la Junta de Andalucía: Prevebús Joven and/or Aprende a Crecer con Seguridad. The total of the surveyed schools represented 230,687 students, with an average of 357.65 students per school.

Measurement Instrument

In order to know the real situation of the schools regarding occupational risk prevention, information was obtained from a self-administered questionnaire addressed to the Head of Studies of primary and secondary education.

The field study was conducted during the first months of 2010. The questionnaire consisted of an introductory part, two main sections and one final section of sociodemographic content, described as follows:

- The introductory part (three questions) served to introduce the subject to the field of study and to obtain the Head of Studies' personal view on the importance of risks prevention and the role conferred to the schools in the task of promoting a culture of prevention.
- The second section (seven questions) dealt with the assessment of occupational safety and health at the schools. It was used to specify the level of predisposition of the people in charge of Andalusian schools towards occupational risk prevention as well as the influencing factors and motivation. Additionally, it attempted to measure actions carried out: adoption, number, kind and periodicity of the measures taken to promote a prevention culture at the school.
- The third section of the questionnaire (five questions) measured the impact of the awareness campaigns specifically designed for these schools (Aprende a Crecer and Prevebús Joven). The knowledge and availability of the materials, guides and studies as well as its effect on both cognitive an behavioural levels of Aprende a Crecer were analyzed. In this case, effective elements were not taken into consideration, as the person being surveyed does not directly receive the impact of the awareness campaign actions.
- Finally, descriptive information related to sex and age of the person surveyed, type of school, province, number of students and levels of education provided was requested.

RESULTS

Assessment of the Public Initiative

Predisposition Towards Promoting a Culture of Prevention
The surveyed subjects considered that the best context to promote a culture of prevention (see Table 1) is the workplace, closely followed by the school and then home. This is a significant result, taking into consideration the increasingly importance that public institutions place on education in occupational risk prevention from the early ages on.

Forty-six percent of the surveyed subjects considered that their schools gave priority to the promotion of a prevention culture among their students. On the contrary, 13% of them saw it as a nonexistent concern at their schools.

There were significant differences when cross tabulating these results with the type of school.

Table 1. Importance of Contexts at Promoting a Prevention Culture

Ranking	Sphere
1st	Work
2nd	School
3rd	Home
4th	University
5th	Mass Media

Privately run schools seemed to give higher priority to promoting prevention, as they showed higher percentages on the scale of importance (quite a lot-much was chosen by 61.9% of the private schools and only by 43.2% of the publicly run ones).

However, it could not be established if the level of importance placed on promoting a prevention culture at schools was linked to the fact of having been visited or not by the programs *Aprende a Crecer* and/or *Prevebús Joven*.

Homes were where schools thought they could exercise the least influence (only 27%), compared to the other three environments under study (work - 36.5%-, school -75%- and leisure time -40%-). In any case, it is necessary to emphasize the self-perceived reduced capacity to influence different social environments except their own schools (approximately 66% of the schools considered that they could exercise a limited influence).

In spite of being the sphere where a bigger influence could be exercised, it is noteworthy that 25% of the schools considered that even in their own sphere, their capacity to influence was null or limited.

From Motivation to Action

As for "Reasons why teachers carry out prevention actions" we find that almost 60% of the surveyed subjects considered that prevention actions were carried out due to the teachers' own beliefs or values. An additional 34% did it because of the high recognition this type of activity had among their colleagues, the school management or both groups (included under the label "Others"). Only six out of one hundred felt themselves forced to take part in prevention activities at their schools.

No differences in behaviour were found between publicly and privately run schools.

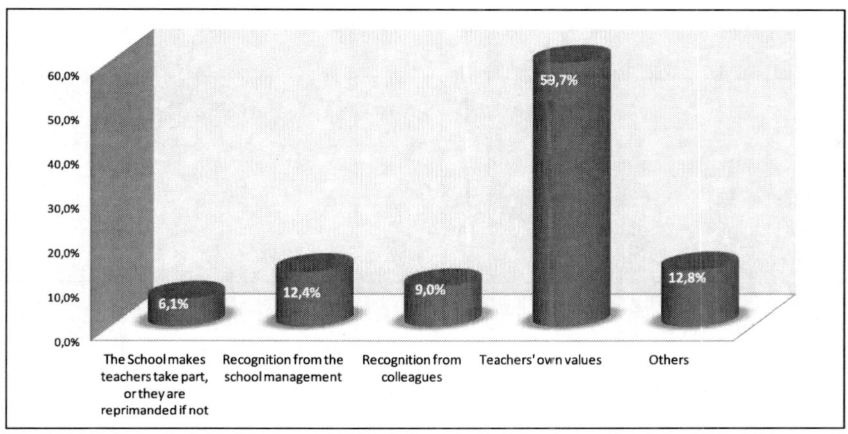

Figure 3. Reasons Why Teachers Carry out Prevention Measures.

The arguments in favour of prevention actions did not seem to change due to the activities promoted by la Junta de Andalucía in relation to these matters (participation in *Prevebús Joven* and *Aprende a Crecer*).

As regards inhibiting factors for carrying out prevention actions, we must remember that only 29 schools did not take any preventive measures and 26 of them gave the reasons for not doing so.

For these schools, an answer was required out of a list of 6 suggested options: "Teachers' lack of problem awareness;" "School management's lack of problem awareness;" "This kind of activities makes teachers' lives more complicated;" "Distrust of the effects on students;" "This kind of activities slows down the development of educational goals;" "There are many social matters that need to be dealt with at schools;" and "Others". Among these, only three were actually chosen. Half of the schools (13) opted for: "There are many social matters that need to be dealt with at schools." The other two reasons are: "Teachers' and school management's lack of problem awareness" (in 4 and 2 cases, respectively). The 5 other cases chose the option "Others" and are of no significant contribution.

If we move to specific actions, 95.9% of those surveyed declared that prevention measurements were being taken at their schools. The content and frequency of these measurements are shown in Table 2.

Only 77 of the surveyed schools (11.5%) had taken part, at least once, in the programme *Aprende a Crecer con Seguridad* by la Junta de Andalucía; it is worth mentioning that 28.6% of them participated in this activity periodically.

Table 2. Measures Taken at Schools. (Absolute Values)

	Never	Only once	Periodically	No answer
1. Participation in the Program "Aprende a Crecer con Seguridad" of la Junta de Andalucía	88%	8.2%	3.3%	0.5%
2. Teacher training in labor risk prevention	35%	36%	28.5%	0.5%
3. Parent training in labor risk prevention	84.5%	11%	4%	0.5%
4. School evacuation plans	2%	9.5%	88%	0.5%
5. Risk evaluation of the school jobs	44%	20.5%	35%	0.5%
6. Taking part in contests, awards, or applying for financial aid to promote a culture of prevention	81%	12.5%	6%	0.5%
7. Visit of Prevebús Joven of Junta de Andalucía	91%	7%	1.5%	0.5%
8. Others: road safety education plans, self-protection plans, etc.	84%	1.5%	14%	0.5%

Almost 65% of the schools admitted to having engaged, at least once, in teacher training activities about risk prevention, although it is also true that, in 55.8% of the cases, this action does not take place periodically but only on specific occasions. Only 15% of the schools have organized parent training activities.

On the other end of the spectrum, practically nine out of ten surveyed subjects declared to develop evacuation plans periodically at their schools. If we try to characterize the schools which do not have these plans (with due caution because of the scarce limited number of observations), we could affirm that they are mainly state primary schools.

Taking part in contests, awards or applying for financial aid to promote a culture of prevention is not a common practice in Andalusian schools: only

18.3% of the schools which declared to take measurements had taken part in this kind of activity on some occasion, and only 32% of them declared doing it on a regular basis.

Eight point five percent of the schools had visited *Prevebús Joven*, and only 21.1% have taken part in it again, thus being this activity the one with the least participation of the analyzed ones.

Assessment of the Public Initiative

Awareness Campaign Aprende a Crecer Con Seguridad

As mentioned before, 11.5% of the surveyed schools took part in the program, *Aprende a Crecer con Seguridad,* and 28.6% of them participated more than once; 92,2% of them are publicly run and the rest are private.

As part of the study, the teachers' opinion about the medium and long term impact of the program on students, from a cognitive as well as a behavioural point of view (see Chart 3) was analyzed.

- Seventy-eight percent of participating schools considered that the campaign, *Aprende a Crecer con Seguridad, was* quite or very useful in raising accident prevention awareness and so promote a culture of prevention among children, parents and teachers.

- One out of two schools surveyed noticed that the students who took part in this activity could quite a lot, or very much better, identify risk situations.

- Forty-two point four percent of surveyed subjects noticed that, after the campaign, students put quite a lot, or very much, into practicing the skills learned about the prevention of risk situations. Forty-four point one percent of them reported that not very much was put into practice.

- Fifty-seven point six percent of subjects surveyed reported that student activity did not seem to be very much safer in the students who took part in the activity. Twenty-seven point one percent of subjects considered student activity to seem quite a lot safer and 3.4% very much safer.

As suggestions for the improvement of the campaign, *Aprende a Crecer con Seguridad*, schools reported:

- It should be extended to all primary education
- It should be done on a periodic basis at all schools
- It should start in September instead of April
- It should be given a wider coverage at the schools
- It should include more activities addressed to families

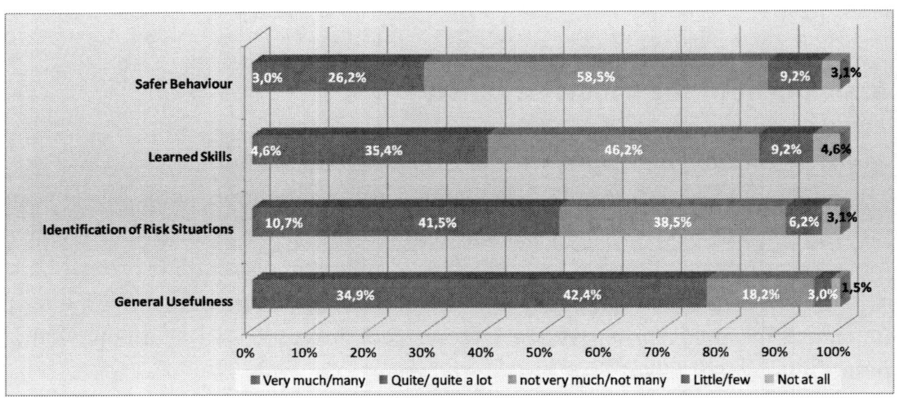

Chart 4. Teachers' Assessment of the Campaign: *Aprende a Crecer con Seguridad.*

Supporting Material of the Campaign, **Aprende a Crecer con Seguridad**

Looking into the knowledge gained and use made by the schools of the primary materials provided by la Junta de Andalucía in order to contribute to the creation of a prevention culture, we highlight the following facts:

- Three out of four schools were unaware of the existence of studies about child accidents; at the other end of the spectrum, only 3.6% declared to know about them and put them into practice.
- Slightly more than 55% did not know about the guide published by la Junta de Andalucía: *La seguridad y salud en el trabajo como materia de enseñanza transversal* (Occupational Safety and Health as Transversal Topic). If we add to this figure the number of schools which knew about this guide but do not have it, the percentage of schools that could not make use of this material increased to a little more than 80%.
- A wider coverage was achieved by the promotional and supporting materials that la Junta de Andalucía prepares about prevention, which were used at a little more than one fourth of the schools. Even so, only 32% of them had these materials (whether used or not).

It is appropriate to accentuate the fact that if we analyze the use of guides, reports and materials among those schools in which they are available (19.8%, 32.1% and 7.1%, respectively), we find that only 57% of schools used the guides, 50% of them used the accident reports, and 80% used promotional materials. The rare use of these guides of transversal topics is worth an additional explanation, as it indicates how seldom prevention was put into practice inside the classroom as a broad and integrating interdisciplinary cross-cutting subject. If we look into the possible relationship between having taken part in the activity *Prevebús Joven* or *Aprende a Crecer con Seguridad*, and the degree of awareness and use of the materials above, we discover that in the case of all three documents, those schools visited showed higher levels of both awareness and use than those schools in which these activities did not take place. Therefore, the support guide published by la Junta de Andalucía, *La seguridad y salud en el trabajo como material de enseñanza transversal,* was used in 20.8% of the visited schools and only in 9.2% of the schools in which the activities did not take place. On the other hand, the promotional and support materials about safety and health are used by 32.1% of the visited schools, value which decreases by 8 percentage points in case of the not visited ones; finally, regarding the studies about child accidents, 7.5% of the visited schools and a very low 2.8% of the not visited ones used them. However, no statistically significant differences were found among publicly and privately run schools.

Campaign Prevebús Joven

Fifty-seven schools took part in this program, 12 of them several times, as mentioned above. The teachers' opinion on the cognitive as well as the behavioural impact of the campaign, mid and long term, was analysed (see Chart 5) with the following results:

- Seventy-two point three percent of the schools which took part in the program, *Prevebús Joven,* considered it quite or very useful in raising safety awareness among adolescents, parents and teachers.
- However, when evaluating its usefulness in the identification of risk situations, 66.0% of the schools reported having noticed not very much or little improvement. Thirty-four percent considered it to be quite or very useful.

- Approximately one of two participants noticed that only sometimes the learned skills were put into practice. Two point one percent of the schools reported that it did not happen at all. Twenty-one point three percent of them thought that the skills are quite or very much put into practice.
- In 76.6% of the cases, the impact on the development of safer behaviour was reported nonexistent or little. On the contrary, 23.4% of the surveyed subjects reported quite a lot of impact.

The surveyed schools made the following suggestions in order to improve the campaign, *Prevebús Joven*:

- It should be extended to a broader domain than work activities.
- The *Prevebús* should stay longer.
- The program should be extended to all students at the school.
- The program should be provided with continuity, so it stops being an occasional activity.
- The vocabulary should be adapted, so the trainers can be better understood by students.
- Students should be allowed to manipulate the materials.

As well as in the case of the program, *Aprende a Crecer con Seguridad*, central tendency and distribution values were calculated in order to make teacher assessment more accurate.

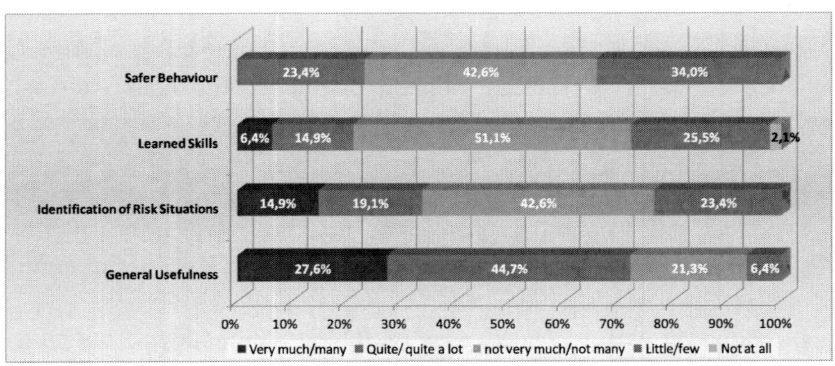

Chart 5. Teachers' Assessment of the Campaign *Prevebús Joven*.

CONCLUSION

We will now summarize the most relevant results (see table 3). Finally, some conclusions will be drawn.

Table 3. Assessment of the Awareness Campaigns at Schools. Summary of the Results

			Aprende a Crecer	*Prevebús Joven*
Participants	Number		11,5%	8,5%
	Frequency		Several Times 28,6%	Several Times 21,1%
	School Profile	Publicly run	92,2%	93%
		Privately run- Run via public and private partnership	7,8%	7%
Impact	Cognitive	Awareness	78%	72%
		Identification of risk situations	50%	35,2%
	Behavioural	Skills put into practice	42,4%	20,3%
		Safe behaviour	30,5%	20,4%

The main reason stated for the lack of action was the wide range of matters of social content to be dealt with at schools. This is the reason given by 50% of the surveyed Head of Studies. Therefore, an interest in cross-cutting themes seemed to be missing from teaching planning and, the fact that only 11.2% of the surveyed schools used the guides to transversal topics must be highlighted. On the other hand, this could be solved if public institutions could succeed in a better integration of actions by simplifying and associating social content. In our particular field of interest, all the educational actions should be integrated in a holistic approach to prevention (health, leisure, risks at home, traffic accidents, labor risks, etc.).

It can be stated that schools were quite skeptical regarding their role as change agents towards a fuller awareness of prevention at the workplace, maybe because they perceived this topic as very distant to the students' present reality. Therefore, better awareness-raising measures for schools must be implemented. Besides, and as mentioned before, education in prevention cannot be conceived as merely adding content, if we want to avoid lack of competence due to an overwhelming amount of information. On the contrary, it must be viewed as related to and integrated into the subjects taught at schools. Consequently, connections between occupational risk prevention and other priority social matters (value education, gender equality, environmental issues…), must be found. It also makes necessary the design of more innovative measures and instruments, instead of limiting prevention culture to specific actions (although also necessary) such as awards or games, for example. As a whole, and according to the teachers' assessment, the analyzed campaigns seem to leave no trace at the schools other than a direct impact on the participating students. No significant relationship was found between a school taking part in these campaigns and its degree of integration of prevention culture and, therefore, its role as change agent. Therefore, the efficiency evaluation of these campaigns must be focused on their direct impact on students. In general, the results of the campaign, *Aprende a Crecer,* were more highly valued by teachers both from a cognitive and from a behavioral point of view, than those of *Prevebús Joven.* As a conclusion, this second campaign seemed to have a poorer design or less successful adaptation to its target audience. On the other hand, and with different degrees, both campaigns were more effective on a cognitive rather than a behavioral level, according to the teachers. In other words, they worked better at raising awareness of the existence of risk and at making students recognize them, rather than at motivating students to adopt safe behavior.

Finally, and as a conclusion, we must say that in spite of the considerable steps taken by schools, as well as public institutions, towards the promotion of initiatives, there is still very much to be done in order to keep supporting the role of schools as change agents within the field of prevention. With this study, we have tried to ascertain and value such a role by identifying possible obstacles, motivations and catalysts of prevention education in schools, as well as to extend a line of research which we hope continues with success in the future.

REFERENCES

Abreu, I. (2006). El pre-test y el post test publicitario: un caso de aplicación a una campaña universitaria de prevención, *UNIrevista*, 1 (3), 11-21.

Agencia Europea para la Seguridad y la Salud en el Trabajo (2006), La integración de la seguridad y la salud en el trabajo en el sistema educativo, Oficina de Publicaciones de de la UE, Belgium.

Araque-Padilla, R., García-Uceda, E., Montero-Simó, M. J. and Rivera-Torres, P. (2010), Determinantes del riesgo psicosocial en el lugar de trabajo: una aplicación empírica a la comunidad andaluza, Actas del XX Congreso nacional de ACEDE, Granada.

Araque-Padilla, R., Montero-Simó, M. J., Carbonero-Ruz, M., Gutiérrez-Villar, B., Melero-Bolaños, R. and Carillo-Castrillo, J. (2011). Una evaluación de la cultura y políticas preventivas en Andalucía, Córdoba, Spain: Publicaciones ETEA.

Burgos, A. (2008). Elementos didácticos y organizativos en la enseñanza de la prevención en el aula, Sevilla: Junta de Andalucía, Consejería de Empleo.

Calero, M.D. and others (2009), Valoración de efectos de la campaña —Aprende a Crecer con Seguridad. Seguimiento y propuestas de actividades de refuerzo, Sevilla: Junta de Andalucía. Consejería de Empleo.

COM. (2002). 118 final. Communication from the Commission. Adapting to change in work and society: a new community strategy on health and safety at work 2002 – 2006, pp. 9. Brussels, Belgium.

European Agency for Safety and Health at Work. (2002). Learning about occupational safety and health. Summary of a seminar organised in Bilbao (4 to 5 March 2002) by the European Agency for Safety and Health at Work and the Spanish EU Presidency in cooperation with the European Commission, in *FORUM*, Number 8.

European Agency for Safety and Health at Work (2004), Mainstreaming occupational safety and health into education. Good practice in school and vocational education, Office for Official Publications of the European Communities.

Hundeloh, H. and Hess, B. (2003), Promoting safety: A component in health promotion in schools, In Injury Control and Safety Promotion, Volume 10, Number 3, September, 165-171.

Junta de Andalucía (2006), I Plan Andaluz de Salud Laboral y Prevención de Riesgos Laborales del personal docente de los centros públicos dependientes de la Consejería de Educación (2006-2010) (BOJA 9th October 2006).

Junta de Andalucía (2004), I Plan General para la Prevención de Riesgos Laborales en Andalucía (2003-2008), (Decreto 313/2003 11th November).

Junta de Andalucía (2010), Estrategia Andaluza de Seguridad y Salud en el Trabajo 2010-2014 (BOJA 24th February 2010).

Montero, M. J., Araque, R. A. and Rey, J. M. (2009), Occupational health and safety in the framework of corporate social responsibility, *Safety Science*, 47, 1440-1445.

Instituto Nacional de Seguridad e Higiene en el Trabajo (2007), Estrategia española de Seguridad y Salud en el Trabajo 2007-2012. Plan de acción para el impulso y ejecución de la estrategia española de seguridad y salud en el trabajo 2007-2012. Documento del Ministerio de Trabajo e Inmigración.

International conference in Rome on occupational safety and health in SME's (2003), Mainstreaming OSH into education: the workers of tomorrow, 1st-3rd October 2003.

Regional Committee for Europe (2007). Health workforce policies in the European Region (European Strategy 2007-2012). In Fifty-seventh session of the WHO. 17th-20th September.

In: Occupational Safety and Health
Editors: I.G. Kavouras, M.C.G. Chalbot

ISBN: 978-1-63117-695-1
© 2014 Nova Science Publishers, Inc.

Chapter 5

OCCUPATIONAL SAFETY IN FINLAND AND SOUTH KOREA

Simo Salminen[1] and Donghyun Seo[2]

[1]Finnish Institute of Occupational Health, Finland
[2]Korea Occupational Safety and Health Agency, South Korea

ABSTRACT

The aim of this review is to compare the occupational safety situation in Finland and South Korea. Research in occupational safety has increased in Korea and should focus on these topics. The occupational accident rate has been higher in Korea than in Finland. What is the reason for this? Korean employees work longer hours than Finnish employees, and longer working hours are related to higher accident rates, and a higher prevalence of depression and suicide. Another considerable difference found between countries was in the safety of small companies and self-employed people.

INTRODUCTION

Finland is a republic in Northern Europe, with a geographical area of 303,892 km^2. The population was 5,375,276 at the end of 2010, which means a population density of 17.69 persons/km^2. The capital city is Helsinki, with 590,000 inhabitants (Statistics Finland, 2011a). South Korea is a republic in

North-east Asia, with a geographical area of 100,033 km^2 (Statistics Korea, 2011a). Population was 49410000 at the end of 2010, which means a population density of 494 persons/km^2. The capital city is Seoul, with 10 million inhabitants (Statistics Korea, 2011b). The significant difference between the two countries lies in the population densities, which in South Korea is almost 25 times that of Finland. The higher population density, the easier it should be to arrange occupational health and safety services..

The number of employed people in Finland in 2010 was 2.4 million (Statistics Finland, 2010). Of these, 68% worked in services, 7% in the construction industry, 22% in manufacturing, and 3% in agriculture and forestry (Elinkeinoelämän keskusliitto, 2011). The number of employed people in South Korea was 23.7 million. Sixty-nine percent of these worked in the service industry; 7.3% in construction; 17.5% in manufacturing; and 5.2% in agriculture, forestry, and fishery (Statistics Korea, 2011c). The proportion of agriculture and forestry, one of the most hazardous industries, is about two times higher in South Korea than in Finland. The share of manufacturing is higher in Finland than in Korea.

Finland had 127,620 occupational accidents in 2009. The accident frequency (accidents per 10,000 employees) was 52.95 at that time. There were 48 fatalities (1.2 per 100,000 employees) (Statistics Finland, 2011b). In Korea, there were 89,459 cases of non-fatal injuries and 1,383 cases of fatal injuries, including those caused by commuting accidents. As for occupational diseases, there were 6,896 non-fatal and 817 fatal cases. The non-fatal injury rate per 100 employees was 0.63 while the fatal injury rate per 100,000 employees was 9.74. The non-fatal injury rate is very low compared to many European countries, whereas the fatal injury rate was very high. This phenomenon is also reflected in the period of treatment as more than 85% of the cases required treatment over 30 days. This means that many minor injury cases were not reported (Kang, 2012). These results mean that the frequency of non-fatal occupational injuries was 1.18 times higher in South Korea than in Finland. The fatality rate of Korea was also 8.1 times higher than that of Finland. The International Labor Office (ILO) collects and estimates the injury rate of all countries. The difference between Finland and South Korea is 5.4 times, both in fatality rate and in non-fatal injury rate. In Finland, the fatality rate was 2.9, and in South Korea it was 15.7 per 100,000 employees, whereas the injury rate was 2,232 per 100,000 workers in Finland and 12,015 in South Korea (Hämäläinen et al., 2006). Among OECD-countries, Korea had the highest fatal accident rate (Nishikitani & Yano, 2008). The gross domestic production (GDP) per capita was not related to the injury rate in OECD-countries (Nasrullah et al., 2008).

The first legislation on occupational safety was created in Finland in 1889. The current legal framework is based on two fundamental laws - the Occupational Safety and Health Act (2002) and the Occupational Health Care Act (1978) (Yrjänheikki & Savolainen, 2000). The Occupational Safety and Health Act is based upon a directive from the European Union. The basic subjects of the Act are workplace risk assessment and a plan for occupational safety. The aim of the law is to prevent all workplace hazards. According to law, the employer has the main responsibility for prevention (Finlex, 2002). A survey given to safety managers and safety representatives of Finnish workplaces showed that the new law has successfully reached workplaces three years after implementation. For example, four out of five companies had conducted both risk assessment and a safety action plan. The law has extended from occupational safety in the manufacturing to the service industry (Salminen et al., 2007). The Act on Occupational Safety and Health Enforcement and Cooperation on Occupational Safety and Health at Workplaces (44/2006) determines the scope of the work of occupational safety inspectors. They have the right to inspect working conditions and to investigate the accidents that occur. The law also gives a framework concerning the co-operation between employer and employees at the workplace (Finlex, 2006).

A survey of workplaces showed that authorities made positive enforcement assessments. The survey also described the effect of assessments on workplace safety and health. The inspectors behaved in a professional manner, and the inspection focuses upon important matters. Also, the inspections led to corrections of infractions (Uusitalo et al., 2012). In Korea, the occupational safety and health system took root as a government policy with the enactment of the Occupational Safety and Health Act in December 1981, and the modification of the enforcement decrees and rules in 1983. Before the enactment of the Occupational Safety and Health Act, ex post facto compensation for insured workers following industrial accidents was the main focus of policy, based on the Industrial Accident Compensation Insurance Act. However, with the passing of the new Act, accident prevention policies were implemented (Yoon, 2011).

With the advent of internationalization and globalization in the 1990s, the scope of occupational safety and health expanded to not only include the safety and health of workers at the workplace, but also to secure the fundamental safety of exported goods and to amend and supplement regulations related to safety and health in preparation for opening the market following the Blue Round and the Uruguay Round. The economic crisis of late 1997 in Korea resulted in downscaling corporate investments in safety and health, and the government implemented systems focused on promoting voluntary corporate activities for accident prevention and on the steady expansion of the climate of disaster prevention as major policies (Yoon, 2011).

The occupational safety and health act consists of seven main chapters: 1) general provisions, 2) the safety and health management system, 3) safety and health management regulations, 4) measures for preventing harms and hazards, 5) the health management of workers, 6) supervision and order, and 7) supplementary provisions (Occupational Safety and Health Act, 2011). The comparison of occupational safety legislation in Finland to that in South Korea is difficult, because the laws are so different. However, commonalities in both legislations include the requirement of a safety manager in the company, and the inspection of machines.

In Finland, accident insurance is based on insurance law, which required accident insurance for all salaried workers. For the self-employed, insurance is voluntary. An employer can purchase insurance from one of 13 competitive, private insurance companies, which is a unique feature of the Finnish system (Tynkkynen, 2012).When an occupational injury occurs, the injured worker reports it to his/her supervisor. The employer makes the compensation claim to the insurance company. The insurance company pays compensation for the salary of an injured worker to the employer. Thus, companies have an economic incentive to make compensation claim (Tynkkynen, 2012). The Finnish official statistics are based on the accepted compensation claims, and its coverage is excellent. There is a special insurance company for farmers, the Farmers' Social Insurance Institution (Mela). Mela handles the statutory pension and employment accident insurance for around 80 000 Finnish farmers. Mela assigns an agent to every farmer, to whom a farmer sends a compensation claim after an occupational injury. In South Korea, the Industrial Accident Compensation Insurance (IACI) has a history of about 50 years. The IACI Act has been revised over 20 times (I. Kim et al., 2012). The system covered over 14.2 million workers in 2010, which included all paid workers as well as atypical workers, such as insurance salespeople, caddies, self-owned ready-mix truck drivers, and visiting teachers specializing in home-school materials. Other social security systems cover 1.5 million workers, including government employees, private teachers, and military personnel (Kang, 2012). There is a semi-government agency, COMWEL (Korea Labor Welfare Corporation) for workers' compensation and welfare service, which administers workers' compensation insurances (COMWEL, 2012). South Korean statistics of occupational accidents and diseases do not include fatalities, injuries, or illnesses at workplaces excluded from IACI coverage: government employees, private school teachers, military personnel, fishermen, workers of small construction projects, self-employed housekeepers, and workers at workplaces with less than five full-time workers in agriculture, forestry (excluding logging), fishery, and hunting (COMWEL, 2012). The comparison of the insurance systems in Finland to that in South Korea is very difficult. The common feature is obligatory insurance for all salaried workers. However, in Korea, one state-supported company issues the insurance, whereas in Finland, it is provided by several private, competing companies. It is rather difficult to estimate the effect of the insurance system on accident rates.

RISK FACTORS OF OCCUPATIONAL INJURIES

Long Working Hours

Korean employees worked longer hours than Finnish employees. The average annual work hours totaled 2,193 in South Korea and 1,697 in Finland (OECD, 2012). Korean researchers recognize the risks of long working hours, as they have found a significantly higher injury rate among employees working over 54 hours per week compared to those working less than 44 hours per week (Lee et al., 2006). Two reviews (Salminen, 2010; Wagstaff et al., 2011) have consistently shown that working over 60 hours per week doubles the risk of occupational injury compared to working 40 hours per week. Studies in the U.S. (Dembe et al., 2005; Dong, 2005; Vegso et al., 2007) and in Canada (Wilkins & Mackenzie, 2007) have indicated that working longer hours linearly increases the risk of occupational injury. A recent American study showed that long working hours increased the risk of occupational injury among women, but not among men (Wirtz et al., 2012).

Sleep Problems

Based on the First Korean Working Condition Survey, J.B. Park and his colleagues (2013) showed that 5.1% of Korean workers had work-related sleep problems. Males, older workers, people with diseases, and shift and night workers more often had sleep problems as compared to the average population. In Finland, sleeptime had decreased by 18 minutes in the past 33 years, and sleep complaints had increased, especially among middle-aged employees (Kronholm et al., 2008). Thus, 22% of Finnish employees suffered from sleep disturbances. Men with disturbed sleep were a significantly higher risk of occupational injury, whereas women with difficulties initiating sleep had an elevated risk of occupational injury (Salminen et al., 2010). Both men and women with trouble sleeping had an increased risk of occupational injury in Canada (Kling et al., 2010) and in the United States (Kessler et al., 2012). Workers with heavy snoring and sleep apnea syndrome even had a two times higher risk of occupational injury in Sweden (Ulfberg et al., 2000; Carter et al., 2003). The comparison of sleep problems in South Korea to that in Finland is challenging, because researchers used different measures in different countries. However, it seems that sleep problems were more common in Finland, although the connection between sleep problems and work is better illustrated in South Korea. It is clear that poor sleep increases the risk of occupational injury.

The Effect of Relatives

There are differences in the effect of relatives upon occupational injury in South Korea and Finland. In Korea, the death of one's parents is the highest stress-giving factor followed by the death of a spouse and close family members. Personal injury was ranked as the sixth in the list (Kang et al., 2008). In Finland, the death or illness of family members was reported to cause sleep disturbances, which doubled the risk of absence from work 19 to 30 months after the event (Vahtera et al., 2006). Depression increased the risk of occupational injury among Korean workers. In a study of small- and medium-sized Korean companies, depressed women had 2.68 times higher risk of occupational injury.

Depressed men had also a 75% higher risk than males without depressive symptoms (Kim et al., 2009a). More than half of injured Korean workers suffered depression. Preoccupations with health, subjective economic stability, self-image, employment status, and alcohol problems significantly predicted depression symptoms (Park, 2011). Among women, change in employment status increased depression symptoms (S.-S. Kim et al., 2012). There are not yet studies on the association between depression and occupational accidents in Finland.

Stress

Because there is no absolute measure of stress, it is not possible to make a direct comparison between Finnish and Korean employees. However, Korean employees working in high-demand jobs had an elevated risk of occupational injury. Among women, low job control and high job strain were stressors increasing the risk of injury (Kim et al., 2009b). Among Finnish hospital workers, psychological distress was not related to occupational accidents. However, low decision latitude, low skill discretion (only for men), and highly monotonous work were stressors predicting occupational injuries. In addition, employees with numerous problems in interpersonal relationships or many collaborative conflicts were more often involved in occupational injuries (Salminen et al., 2003). Although it is not possible to have a direct comparison between Korean and Finnish studies, low autonomy in work was a common stress factor leading to occupational injury in those countries.

Handedness

An examination of all children born in 1966 in Northern Finland showed that at the age of 31, 7.9% of men and 6.1% of women were left-handed, whereas 1.7% of men and 0.9% of women were ambidextrous. There is no difference between right- and left-handers in injury involvement (Pekkarinen & Anttonen, 2000). However, later, based on the same data set, we found that ambidextrous men had a slightly higher risk of traffic and home injury, whereas ambidextrous women faced a slightly elevated risk of work injury (Pekkarinen et al., 2003).

In a study of 2,437 Koreans, 5.8% were left-handed and 7.9% were ambidextrous. Males were left-handed slightly more often than females. Right-handed and ambidextrous people used their right hand in actions requiring accuracy more often, whereas left-handers used their left hand more often when making a forceful action. Left-handed people were overrepresented among injury victims (Jung & Jung, 2009). The proportion of ambidextrous people in Korea is higher than in Finland, one of the highest rates in the world. However, ambidextrous people injured themselves more often than left-handers in Finland, whereas in Korea, left-handers were involved in injuries more often than people who used both hands equally.

Suicides

The suicide rate in Korea (men 30.3 per 100,000 inhabitants, women 13.0, Kwon et al., 2009) is higher than it is in Finland (17.8) (Statistics Finland, 2011c). Korea has the highest annual suicide rate in the world, which is partly explained by working too hard. The Japanese have a distinct term for overwork suicide "karo jisatsu" (Targum & Kitanaka, 2012). The economic crises1997/1998 increased the suicide mortality in South Korea (Kwon et al., 2009). However, Finland, which experienced a rising unemployment rate in the deep economic recession during the 1990s, did not show an increase in their suicide rate (Ostamo & Lönnqvist, 2001). The last economic crisis, in 2008, increased the suicide rate of the working age population in Finland (Stuckler et al., 2011). Suicides at the workplace are a very rare phenomenon and often misclassified. In California only 82% of workplace suicide cases were classified in the right manner (Kraus et al., 2005). In South Korea, 12 out of 2,996 patients of self-inflicted injury had attempted suicide at their workplace (C.A. Lee et al., 2012). In Finland, there is no such published information. Sales and service workers, machine operators (Lee & Ha, 2011), and farmers (Lee et al., 2010) had an elevated risk of suicide in South Korea. However, being a victim of occupational injury increased suicidal ideation (Kuo et al., 2012).

Weather

In Korean workplaces, the problem is the hot climate. Human performance suffers in demanding environments. Accurate perception and good motor skills decrease significantly in temperatures ranging from 30-33°C (Ramsey & Kwon, 1992). Injuries also increase when temperatures grows over 32°C (Fogleman et al., 2005). In the US, most injuries occurred during the warm and humid months on tankers travelling along the Mississippi River (Ghahramani, 1999). The occupational accident rates in Korea were changed with weather conditions such as heavy snow, heavy rain, and wind (Kim, 2011). In Finland, cold weather is a problem at workplaces situated outside. Temperatures below -7°C increased the risk of occupational injury (Fogleman et al., 2005). In Ohio, the injury rate was over 70 times higher on days when the average temperature decreased below 0°F than that of days with an average of more than 19°F. The injury rate even increased when wind speed exceeded 20 mph (Sinks et al., 1987). In the American mining industry, the strongest association between cold temperature and injuries was found when the temperature was 29°F or below (Hassi et al., 2000). Climate change (Kjellstrom, 2012) affects occupational safety both in Finland and in South Korea. In Korea, the number of hot days may increase and serious heat stress is possible during the hot season. In Finland, the number of cold days will decrease, which may improve occupational safety.

ORGANIZATIONAL RISK FACTORS

Temporary Work

In South Korea, 21% of employees have a temporary contract with their employer (Statistics Korea, 2011b). In Finland, 16% of employees had a fixed-term contract in 2007, but 53% of new contracts were also fixed-term (Statistics Finland, 2007). However, a temporary contract may not mean the exact same thing in South Korea as in Finland. According to a large review, 76 out of 93 studies showed that precarious employment was associated with deterioration in occupational health and safety (Quinlan et al., 2001). Another review indicated an increased risk of occupational injury among temporary workers (Virtanen et al., 2005). Based on three large empirical data sets, Saloniemi and Salminen (2010) showed that fixed-term workers in Finland were not more exposed to occupational injuries than permanent workers. However, they encountered physical violence or a threat of violence at work significantly more often than permanent workers (Salminen & Saloniemi, 2010). A more recent empirical study showed that accident risks are increasing in temporary agency work in Finland (Hintikka, 2011). In a study from South Korea, employees with temporary contracts had over twice the number of occupational injuries compared to permanent workers (Im et al., 2012). We can conclude that the majority of studies have indicated a higher risk of occupational injury among temporary workers.

Unemployment

The unemployment rate is higher in Finland (8.4%) than in Korea (3.7%), and the difference is higher for long-term unemployment (23.6% vs. 0.3%) (OECD, 2012). When a high unemployment rate is a sign of economic recession, it usually means a lower occupational accident rate (Boone & van

Ours, 2006; Boone et al., 2011); however, no meaningful connection was found between fatal accidents and business cycles in Finland (Saloniemi & Oksanen, 1998).

Migration

In Finland, there were 177,000 immigrants in 2010, which was 5% of the entire population. The proportion of immigrants in the workforce was 3.5% at the end of 2009 (Reini, 2012). In South Korea, there were 1,261,415 immigrants in 2010, which was 2.5% of the entire population (Korea Immigration Service, 2011). The proportion of immigrants in the workforce was 3.1% at the end of 2010 (Hyundai Research Institute, 2011). Thus, immigrants made a stronger contribution to the Finnish national economy than to the Korean economy. According to a review of 31 studies, foreign-born workers were over two times more often involved in occupational injuries than native workers (Salminen, 2011). However, in Finland, immigrant bus drivers did not encounter more occupational injuries than Finnish drivers (Salminen et al., 2009). One out of three Korean-Chinese migrant workers suffered depression and female workers had a higher depression scores than male workers (H. Lee et al., 2012).

Size of Company

Finnish (Salminen, 1993; Pukkila, 1994) studies have found that accident frequency is highest in middle-sized companies with 31-50 employees. Accident frequency is lower in both smaller companies (with less than 5 employees) and larger companies (over 250 employees). In the manufacturing industry of Korea, companies with less than 10 employees showed a 9.3 times higher injury rate than companies with over 1,000 employees (Jeong, 1997), and in the construction industry, small companies with under 10 employees had a non-fatal injury rate about three times and death rate two times that of those with over 1,000 employees (Jeong, 1998). Larger companies tend to have a lower injury rate than the smaller ones in Korea (Jeong, 1997, 1998, 1999; Im et al., 2009). In the Danish construction industry, however, there was an inverse relationship between firm size and serious fall injuries and a direct relationship between firm size and minor injury rates (Kines & Mikkelsen, 2003). This inverse relationship between firm size and accident frequency was also found in Italian industry (Fabiano et al., 2004). In the US. small establishments with under 50 employees were suspected of underreporting their injuries (Oleinick et al., 1995; Dong et al., 2011).

Construction Industry

There were 3,028 fatalities and 125,929 non-fatal injuries in the construction industry of Korea in the years 1991-1994. The fatality rate in construction was 23.5 per 100,000 per year, and the total injury rate was 1.55% (Jeong, 1998). Falling from a height caused over half (53%) of fatalities. In addition, deaths due to structural collapse and electric shock were significantly higher than in other industries (Im et al., 2009). A mobile sensing device was developed in Korea to warn workers about hazardous situations at construction sites (Lee et al., 2009). In the Finnish construction industry, the accident rate was 70 injuries per million working hours, which is lower than that in South Korea. Subcontractor workers had a higher risk of serious injury than workers of main contractors (Salminen, 1995). There were relatively more accidents at construction sites for blocks of flats than at construction sites for terraced houses (Niskanen & Saarsalmi, 1983). A Finnish-based Cochrane review showed that a multifaceted safety campaign and a multifaceted drug program are effective ways to prevent construction injuries (Lehtola et al., 2008).

Metal Industry

In the Korean manufacturing industry, electronics consist of 15%, machinery 13%, and automobiles 12% of production (Kang, 2011). The occupational accident rate in the metal industry was 38.8 per 1,000 workers, which is the highest of the manufacturing industries (Park et al., 2002). In Finland, there is no epidemiological study on occupational injuries in the metal industry. In the metal product industry, injuries were more frequent during maintenance tasks (Saari & Rinne, 1977; Saari & Lahtela, 1981). Positive feedback related to housekeeping reduced 70% to 90% of injuries in a Finnish shipyard (Saari & Näsänen, 1989). In the metal workshop of the Finnish state railway company, when positive feedback based on the housekeeping index increased from 57% to 89%, sick leaves decreased from 12.8% to 9.9% (Laitinen et al., 1997). In another engineering workshop with a participatory ergonomic process, absenteeism decreased by 25% (Laitinen et al., 1998a). A high safety index was related to a low accident rate in 51 metal product manufacturing companies (Laitinen et al. 1998b; Laitinen et al., 1999).

Forest Industry

The number of injuries in the Korean forest industry was 2,164 in 2010, which represented 2.8% of the total accident rate and represented the second highest accident rate following the mining industry (8.6%). Korea's terrain is mostly mountainous, and not arable. Mountains make up about two-thirds of the total land area. Workplaces in the forest industry in Korea are very steep and extensive, which means that forest workers face dangers and difficulties to work and move. Sometimes, workers can slip on wet land due to low vegetation, which disturbs movement, and can be bitten by bees or snakes (Choi, 2011). The Korean government has invested in managing public forests to reduce greenhouse gas and increase jobs for the poor living in rural and mountainous areas. In 2009, workers with less than one-year of experience in forest work accounted for 96% of total injuries in that field and most accidents occurred during logging season (Lim, 2010). Agriculture and forestry are the most hazardous industries in Finland, because 17% of the workers had injuries during a 12 month period (Grönqvist et al., 2010). The main causes of forestry accidents were losing one's balance, encountering a small flying object, and the chain saw. The most typical work phases in which accidents occurred were delimbing and felling (Salminen et al., 2001). Risk taking was not related to the accidents of forestry workers (Salminen et al., 1999). However, the results were contradictory related to the effectiveness of personal protection equipment of loggers (Klen, 1997). Safety boots prevented the greatest number of injuries (Klen & Väyrynen, 1984). The accident rate of the forestry industry in Finland is higher than that in South Korea. In Finland, the rate is based on forestry workers´ self-reports, whereas in Korea the rate is based on compensation claims to the insurance company.

Agriculture

The fatality rate in agriculture is higher in South Korea (0.3 per 1,000 per annum, S.-J. Lee et al., 2012) than in Finland (0.1, Rautiainen et al., 2009). The injury rate among Finnish farmers is more than twice that of all employees on average. Crop production (Sinisalo, 2012) and animal husbandry (Taattola et al., 2012) had the highest risk of occupational injury. Machine use was the most common cause of accidents among male Korean farmers; whereas, for female farmers, falling was the most common type of injury (S.-J. Lee et al., 2012).

Self-Employed Persons

The proportion of the self-employed in the work force was higher in South Korea (28.8%) than in Finland (13.5%) (OECD, 2012). Self-employed workers had an almost 40% higher accident frequency than salaried workers in Finland (Pukkila, 1998). Also, in the U.S., self-employed workers were 2.7 times more likely to be victims of fatal work injuries than their salaried counterparts (Pegula, 2004). In Korea, the accidents of self-employed people are not included in occupational accidents. Thus, we cannot conduct a comparison between Finland and Korea in the accident rate of the self-employed.

Violence at Work

Finnish employees encountered violence in their work more often than Korean workers. In Finland, 4% of employees had experienced physical violence and another 4% had experienced verbal aggression (Grönqvist et al., 2010), whereas in South Korea, 0.9% of employees had encountered physical violence and 0.8% verbal violence (Choi et al., 2010). Based on Finnish national victimization surveys, violence at work had increased from 2% to 5% in the time period of 1988-2003 (Heiskanen, 2007). Analysis of Finnish national accident statistics showed that occupational accidents related to violence increased to as much as 35% from 2003 to 2006 (Hintikka & Saarela, 2010). Especially, violence against women had increased. The most hazardous occupations were those of prison guards, police officers, and mental health nurses (Salminen, 1997). The same occupations are still the most hazardous for men, whereas for women medical and nursing work, social work, pedagogic work, and child day-care work had the highest risk of violence (Heiskanen, 2007; Hintikka & Saarela, 2010). Encountering violence at work increased alcohol consumption and psychological distress among police officers (Leino et al., 2012).

Injury Rehabilitation

In South Korea, male, middle-aged, and college-educated employees were more likely to return to work after occupational injury. Employees with mild disabilities were employed more often in a different firm, while those with moderate disabilities were relatively more likely to become self-employed (Park, 2012). In Finland, early part-time sick leave provided a faster and more sustainable return to work after a musculoskeletal disorder. The total sickness absence during a 12-month follow-up period was about 20% lower for injured employees with part-time sick leave (Viikari-Juntura et al., 2012). Among New Zealand workers, three months after the work injury, employees with low income, physical work tasks, temporary employment, long week schedules, obesity, and hospital admission were more likely not to be at work (Lilley et al., 2012). Injury severity and the ability to cope with accidental injury were the best predictors of return to work in the long term among Swiss employees (Hepp et al., 2011).

CONCLUSION

Based on the above review we may conclude that:

1. The accident rate in South Korea is several times higher than that in Finland. However, Finnish employees encounter violence in their work more often than Korean employees.
2. The most significant difference between Finland and South Korea is that Koreans work longer hours than their Finnish colleagues. Longer work hours increased the risk of occupational injury. Perhaps, it also increases depression and suicides among Korean workers.
3. Among organizational factors, the safety of self-employed and of those in small companies distinguished Finland and South Korea. In Korea, small companies had the highest injury rate, whereas middle-sized Finnish companies had the highest frequency of occupational injuries. In Finland, self-employed workers had a higher injury rate than salaried employees, but this information is not currently available for Korea.
4. Research on occupational safety has increased in South Korea during the recent past. Future research should be focused on the effect of

longer work hours upon occupational injury, and occupational safety in small companies and among self-employed people.

REFERENCES

Boone, J., & van Ours, J. C. (2006). Are recessions good for workplace safety? *Journal of Health Economics*, 25, 1069-1093.

Boone, J., van Ours, J. C., Wuellrich, J.-P., & Zweimüller, J. (2011). Recessions are bad for workplace safety. *Journal of Health Economics*, 30, 764-773.

Carter, N., Ulfberg, J., Nyström, B., & Edling, C. (2003). Sleep debt, sleepiness and accidents among males in the general population and male professional drivers. *Accident Analysis and Prevention*, 35, 613-617.

Choi, E. S., Jung, H.-S., Kim, S.-H., & Park, H. (2010). The influence of workplace violence on work-related anxiety and depression experience among Korean employees. *Journal of Korean Academy of Nursing*, 40, 650-661.

Choi, H. S. (2011). Examples focused on workplace to prevent accidents at forest work. *Sanrimji*, 11, 106-107.

COMWEL. (2012). http://www.kcomwel.or.kr/eng/intr/welc_idx.jsp. (accessed on 18.05.2012)

Dembe, A. E., Erickson, J. B., Delbos, R. G., & Banks, S. M. (2005). The impact of overtime and long work hours on occupational injuries and illnesses: new evidence from the United States. *Occupational and Environmental Medicine*, 62, 588-597.

Dong, X. (2005). Long workhours, work scheduling and work-related injuries among construction workers in the United States. *Scandinavian Journal of Work, Environment & Health*, 31, 329-335.

Dong, X. S., Fujimoto, A., Ringen, K., Stafford, E., Platner, J. W., Gittleman, J. L., & Wang, X. (2011). Injury underreporting among small establishments in the construction industry. *American Journal of Industrial Medicine*, 54, 339-349.

Elinkeinoelämän keskusliitto. (2011). Suomen elinkeinorakenne, osuus kokonaistuotannosta, % (The industries in Finland, the share of national production). 12.9.2011/rak2/jka/EKI Talousgraafit. (in Finnish)

Fabiano, B., Curró, F., & Pastorino, R. (2004). A study of the relationship between occupational injuries and firm size and type in the Italian industry. *Safety Science*, 42, 587-600.

Finlex. (2002). Työturvallisuuslaki, 23.8.2002/738. (Law of occupational safety) http://www.finlex.fi/fi/laki/ajantasa/2002/20020738. Retrieved: 25.4.2012. (in Finnish)

Finlex. (2006). Laki työsuojelun valvonnasta ja työpaikan työsuojeluyhteistoiminnasta, 20.1.2006/44 (The occupational safety and health enforcement act). http://www.finlex.fi/fi/laki/ajantasa/2006/20060044. Retrieved: 18.5.2012. (in Finnish)

Fogleman, M., Fakhrzadeh, L., & Bernard, T. E. (2005). The relationship between outdoor thermal conditions and acute injury in an aluminum smelter. *International Journal of Industrial Ergonomics*, 35, 47-55.

Ghahramani, B. (1999). An analysis of work environments and operations in hot and humid areas. *International Journal of Occupational Safety and Ergonomics*, 5, 591-596.

Grönqvist, R., Mattila, S., & Salminen, S. (2010). Työtapaturmat (Occupational injuries). In T. Kauppinen et al. (Eds.), Työ ja terveys Suomessa 2009 (pp. 109-117). Helsinki: Työterveyslaitos. (in Finnish).

Hassi, J., Gardner, L., Hendricks, S., & Bell, J. (2000). Occupational injuries in the mining industry and their association with statewide cold ambient temperatures in the USA. *American Journal of Industrial Medicine*, 38, 49-58.

Heiskanen, M. (2007). Violence at work in Finland; Trends, contents, and prevention. *Journal of Scandinavian Studies in Criminology and Crime Prevention*, 8, 22-40.

Hepp, U., Moergeli, H., Buchi, S., Bruchhaus-Steinert, H., Sensky, T., & Schnyder, U. (2011). The long-term prediction of return to work following serious accidental injuries: A follow up study. *BMC Psychiatry*, 11(1), 53.

Hintikka, N. (2011). Accidents at work during temporary agency work in Finland - Comparisons between certain major industries and other industries. *Safety Science*, 49, 473-483.

Hintikka, N., & Saarela, K. L. (2010). Accidents at work related to violence - Analysis of Finnish national accident statistics database. *Safety Science*, 48, 517-525.

Hyundai Research Institute. (2011). VIP Report 11-07 (No. 477). (in Korean).

Hämäläinen, P., Takala, J., & Saarela, K. L. (2006). Global estimates of occupational accidents. *Safety Science*, 44, 137-156.

Im, H.-J., Kwon, Y.-J., Kim, S.-G., Kim, Y.-K., Ju, Y.-S., & Lee, H.-P. (2009). The characteristics of fatal occupational injuries in Korea's construction industry, 1997-2004. *Safety Science*, 47, 1159-1162.

Im, H.-J., Oh, D.-G., Ju, Y.-S., Kwon, Y.-J., Jang, T.-W., & Yim, J. (2012). The association between nonstandard work and occupational injury in Korea. *American Journal of Industrial Medicine*, 55, 876-883. doi: 10.1002/ajim.22055.

Jeong, B. Y. (1997). Characteristics of occupational accidents in the manufacturing industry of South Korea. *International Journal of Industrial Ergonomics*, 20, 301-306.

Jeong, B. Y. (1998). Occupational deaths and injuries in the construction industry. *Applied Ergonomics*, 29, 355-360.

Jeong, B. Y. (1999). Comparisons of variables between fatal and nonfatal accidents in manufacturing industry. *International Journal of Industrial Ergonomics*, 23, 565-572.

Jung, H. S., & Jung, H.-S. (2009). Hand dominance and hand use behaviour reported in a survey of 2437 Koreans. *Ergonomics*, 52, 1362-1371.

Kang, S. K. (2011). Occupational safety and health profile in Korea. *Asian-Pacific Newsletter on Occupational Health and Safety*, 18, 55-57.

Kang, S. K. (2012). The current status and the future of occupational safety and health in Korea. Industrial Health, 59, 12-16.

Kang, Y., Hahm, H., Yang, S., & Kim, T. (2008). Application of the life change unit model for the prevention of accident proneness among small to medium sized industries in Korea. *Industrial Health*, 46, 470-476.

Kessler, R. C., Berglund, P. A., Coulouvrat, C., Fitzgerald, T., Hajak, G., Roth, T., Shahly, V., Shillington, A. C., Stephenson, J. J., & Walsh, J. K. (2012). Insomnia, comorbidity, and risk of injury among insured Americans: Results from the America Insomnia Survey. *Sleep*, 35, 825-834.

Kim, H.-C., Park, S.-G., Min, K.-B., & Yoon, K.-J. (2009a). Depressive symptoms and self-reported occupational injury in small and medium-sized companies. *International Archives of Occupational and Environmental Health*, 82, 715-721.

Kim, H.-C., Min, J.-Y., Min, K.-B., & Park, S.-G. (2009b). Job strain and the risk for occupational injury in small- to medium-sized manufacturing enterprises: A prospective study of 1,209 Korean employees. *American Journal of Industrial Medicine*, 52, 322-330.

Kim, I., Rhie, J., Yoon, J.-D., Kim, J., & Won, J. (2012). Current situation and issue of industrial accident compensation insurance. *Journal of Korean Medical Sciences*, 27, S47-S54.

Kim, S.-S., Subramanian, S. V., Sorensen, G., Perry, M. J., & Christiani, D. C. (2012). Association between change in employment status and new-onset depressive symptoms in South Korea - a gender analysis. *Scandinavian Journal of Work, Environment & Health*, 38, 537-545. doi:10.5271/sjweh.3286.

Kim, Y. S. (2011). Weather and occupational accident. *OSH Research Brief*, 5(2), 30-35. (in Korean)

Kines, P., & Mikkelsen, K. L. (2003). Effects of firm size on risks and reporting of elevation fall injury in construction trades. *Journal of Occupational and Environmental Medicine*, 45, 1074-1078.

Kjellstrom, T. (2012). Occupational health aspects of climate change. Paper presented at the 30th International Congress on Occupational Health in Cancun, Mexico, March 18-23.

Klen, T. (1997). Personal protectors and working behaviour of loggers. *Safety Science*, 25, 89-103.

Klen, T., & Väyrynen, S. (1984). The role of personal protection in the prevention of accidental injuries in logging work. *Journal of Occupational Accidents*, 6, 263-275.

Kling, R. N., McLeod, C. B., & Koehoorn, M. (2010). Sleep problems and workplace injuries in Canada. *Sleep*, 33, 611-618.

Korea Immigration Service. (2011). KIS Statistics 2010. Seoul: Ministry of Justice. (in Korean)

Kraus, J. F., Schaffer, K., Chu, L., & Rice, T. (2005). Suicides at work: Misclassification and prevention implications. *International Journal of Occupational and Environmental Health*, 11, 246-253.

Kronholm, E., Partonen, T., Laatikainen, T., Peltonen, M., Härmä, M., Hublin, C., Kaprio, J., Aro, A. R., Partinen, M., Fogelholm, M., Valve, R., Vahtera, J., Oksanen, T., Kivimäki, M., Koskenvuo, M., & Sutela, H. (2008). Trends in self-reported sleep duration and insomnia-related symptoms in Finland from 1972 to 2005: a comparative review and re-analysis of Finnish population samples. *Journal of Sleep Research*, 17, 54-62.

Kuo, C.-Y., Liao, S.-C., Lin, K.-H., Wu, C.-L., Lee, M.-B., Guo, N.-W., & Guo, Y .L. (2012). Predictors for suicidal ideation after occupational injury. *Psychiatry Research*, 198, 430-435 doi:10.1016/j.psychres.2012.02.011.

Kwon, J.-W., Chun, H., & Cho, S.-I. (2009). A closer look at the increase in suicide rates in South Korea from 1986-2005. *BMC Public Health*, 9(72), 1-9.

Laitinen, H., Saari, J. & Kuusela, J. (1997). Initiating an innovative change process for improved working conditions and ergonomics with participation and performance feedback: A case study in an engineering workshop. *International Journal of Industrial Ergonomics*, 19, 299-305.

Laitinen, H., Saari, J., Kivistö, M., & Rasa, P.-L. (1998a). Improving physical and psychosocial working conditions through a participatory ergonomic process. A before-after study at an engineering workshop. *International Journal of Industrial Ergonomics*, 21, 35-45.

Laitinen, H., Rasa, P.-L., Räsänen, T., & Nykyri, E. (1998b). An observation method as a tool for workplace risk assessment. *Technology, Law and Insurance*, 3, 57-61.

Laitinen, H., Rasa, P.-L., Räsänen, T., Lankinen, T., & Nykyri, E. (1999). ELMERI observation method for predicting the accident rate and the absence due to sick leaves. *American Journal of Industrial Medicine, Supplement* 1, 86-88.

Lee, C. A., Choi, S. C., Jung, K. Y., Cho, S. H., Lim, K. Y., Pai, K. S., & Cho, J. P. (2012). Characteristics of patients who visit the emergency department with self-inflicted injury. *Journal of Korean Medical Science*, 27, 307-312.

Lee, H., Ahn, H., Miller, A., Gi Park, C., & Kim, S. J. (2012). Acculturative stress, work-related psychosocial factors and depression in Korean-Chinese migrant workers in Korea. *Journal of Occupational Health*, 54, 206-214.

Lee, K. S., Kim, H., Chang, S. H., Jung-Choi, K.-H., Oh, W. K., Choi, J. W., Yi, K. H., & Oh, J. Y. (2006). Relationship between injury occurrence and workplace organization in small-sized manufacturing factories. *Korean Journal of Occupational and Environmental Medicine*, 18, 73-86.

Lee, S.-J., Kim, I., Ryou, H., Lee, K.-S., & Kwon, Y.-J. (2012). Work-related injuries and fatalities among farmers in South Korea. *American Journal of Industrial Medicine,* 55, 76-83.

Lee, U.-K., Kim, J.-H., Cho, H., & Kang, K.-I. (2009). Development of a mobile safety monitoring system for construction sites. *Automation in Construction*, 18, 258-264.

Lee, W., & Ha, J. (2011). The association between nonstandard employment and suicidal ideation: Data from the First~Fourth Korea National Health and Nutrition Examination surveys. *Korean Journal of Occupational and Environmental Medicine*, 23, 89-97.

Lee, W. J., Cha, E. S., & Moon, E. K. (2010). Disease prevalence and mortality among agricultural workers in Korea. *Journal of Korean Medical Science*, 25, s112-s118.

Lehtola, M. M., van der Molen, H. F., Lappalainen, J., Hoonakker, P. L. T., Hsiao, H., Haslam, R. A., Hale, A. R., & Verbeek, J. H. (2008). The effectiveness of interventions for preventing injuries in the construction industry. A systematic review. *American Journal of Preventive Medicine*, 35, 77-85.

Leino, T., Eskelinen, K., Summala, H., & Virtanen, M. (2012). Injuries caused by work-related violence: Frequency, need for medical treatment and associations with adverse mental health and alcohol use among Finnish police officers. *American Journal of Industrial Medicine*, 55, 691-697. doi: 10.1002/ajim.22026.

Lilley, R., Davie, G., Ameratunga, S. & Derrett, S. (2012). Factors predicting work status 3 months after injury: results from the prospective outcomes of injury study. *BMJ Open* 2, 2, e00400

Lim, T. Y. (2010). Causes and preventions of accidents in forest industry. *Sanrimji*, 4, 104-105. (in Korean)

Mela. (no year). Insured wellbeing from Mela. Espoo: Farmers' Social Insurance Institution.

Nasrullah, M., Laflamme, L., & Khan, J. (2008). Does economic level similarly matter for injury mortality in the OECD and non-OECD countries? *Safety Science*, 46, 784-791.

Nishikitani, M., & Yano, E. (2008). Differences in the lethality of occupational accidents in OECD countries. *Safety Science*, 46, 1078-1090.

Niskanen, T., & Saarsalmi, O. (1983). Accident analysis in the construction of buildings. *Journal of Occupational Accidents*, 5, 89-98.

Occupational safety and health act. no. 10968. 2011. http://english.kosha.or.kr/main. (accessed on 14.05.2012)

OECD. (2012). OECD factbook 2011-2012. Http://dx.doi.org/10.1787/csp-fin-table-2011-1-en. and http://dx.doi.org/10.1787/csp-kor-table-2011-1-en. Last updated: 18 January 2012.

Oleinick, A., Gluck, J. V., & Guire, K. E. (1995). Establishment size and risk of occupational injury. *American Journal of Industrial Medicine*, 28, 1-21.

Ostamo, A., & Lönnqvist, J. (2001). Attempted suicide rates and trends during a period of severe economic recession in Helsinki, 1989-1997. *Social Psychiatry and Psychiatric Epidemiology*, 36, 354-360.

Park, H., Ha, E., Kim, J., Jung, H., & Paek, D. (2002). Occupational health services for small-scale enterprises in Korea. *Industrial Health*, 40, 1-6.

Park, J. B., Nakata, A., Swanson, N. G., & Chun, H. (2013). Organizational factors associated with work-related sleep problems in a nationally representative sample of Korean workers. *International Archive of*

Occupational and Environmental Health, 86, 211-222 doi: 10.1007/s00420-012-0759-3.

Park, S. K. (2011). Exploration of the prevalence and correlates of depression among South Korean workers with injuries. *Work*, 39, 345-351.

Park, S. K. (2012). Associations of demographic and injury-related factors with return to work among job-injured workers with disabilities in South Korea. *Journal of Rehabilitation Medicine*, 44, 473-476.

Pegula, S. M. (2004). Occupational fatalities: self-employed workers and wage and salary workers. *Monthly Labor Review*, 127 (3), 30-40.

Pekkarinen, A., & Anttonen, H. (2000). Pohjois-Suomessa syntyneiden tapaturmat 30 ikävuoteen saakka. *Työ ja ihminen*, 14, 15-26. (in Finnish)

Pekkarinen, A., Salminen, S., & Järvelin, M.-R. (2003). Hand preference and risk of injury among the Northern Finland birth cohort at the age of 30. *Laterality*, 8, 339-346.

Pukkila, P. (1994). Työelämän suurimmat tapaturmariskit keskisuurissa yrityksissä (The highest injury risks in the worklife in the middle-sized companies). *Tapaturmavakuutus*, 67 (2), 8-9. (in Finnish)

Pukkila, P. (1998). Yrittäjillä selvästi suurempi tapaturmariski kuin työntekijöillä (Self-employed had a greater injury risk than workers). *Tapaturmavakuutus*, 71 (3), 10-11. (in Finnish)

Quinlan, M., Mayhew, C., & Bohle, P. (2001). The global expansion of precarious employment, work disorganization, and consequences for occupational health: a review of recent research. *International Journal of Health Services*, 31, 335-414.

Ramsey, J. D., & Kwon, Y. G. (1992). Recommended alert limits for perceptual motor loss in hot environments. *International Journal of Industrial Ergonomics*, 9, 245-257.

Rautiainen, R. H., Ledolter, J., Donham, K. J., Ohsfeldt, R. L., & Zwerling, C. (2009). Risk factors for serious injury in Finnish agriculture. *American Journal of Industrial Medicine*, 52, 419-428.

Reini, K. (2012). Maahanmuuton taloudelliset vaikutukset. Vieraskielisen työvoiman aluetaloudelliset vaikutukset Pohjanmaalle (The economic effects of immigration. The regional economic effects of immigrant labour on Ostrobotnia). Report 12/2012. Helsinki: National Institute for Health and Welfare. (in Finnish)

Saari, J., & Rinne, R. (1977). Accidents and working conditions in two industrial branches with different accident rates. *Control*, 4, 11-17.

Saari, J., & Lahtela, J. (1981). Work conditions and accidents in three industries. *Scandinavian Journal of Work, Environment and Health*, 7 (suppl 4), 97-105.

Saari, J., & Näsänen, M. (1989). The effect of positive feedback on industrial housekeeping and accidents; a long-term study at a shipyard. *International Journal of Industrial Ergonomics*, 4, 201-211.

Salminen, S. (1993). The effect of company size on serious occupational accidents. In R. Nielsen, & K. Jörgensen (Eds.), Advances in Industrial Ergonomics and Safety V (pp. 507-514). London: Taylor & Francis.

Salminen, S. (1995). Serious occupational accidents in the construction industry. *Construction Management and Economics*, 13, 299-306.

Salminen, S. (1997). Violence in the workplaces in Finland. *Journal of Safety Research*, 28, 123-131.

Salminen, S. (2010). Shift work and extended working hours as risk factors for occupational injury. *Ergonomics Open Journal*, 3, 14-18.

Salminen, S. (2011). Are immigrants at increased risk of occupational injury? A literature review. *Ergonomics Open Journal*, 4, 139-144.

Salminen S., Kivimäki, M., Elovainio, M., & Vahtera, J. (2003). Stress factors predicting injuries of hospital personnel. *American Journal of Industrial Medicine*, 44, 32-36.

Salminen, S., Klen, T., & Ojanen, K. (1999). Risk taking and accident frequency among Finnish forestry workers. *Safety Science*, 33, 143-153.

Salminen, S., Klen, T., & Ojanen, K. (2001). Epidemiology of occupational accidents of Finnish forestry workers. *Journal of Forest Science*, 47, 42-44.

Salminen, S., Oksanen, T., Vahtera, J., Sallinen, M., Härmä, M., Salo, P., Virtanen, M., & Kivimäki, M. (2010). Sleep disturbances as a predictor of occupational injuries among public sector workers. *Journal of Sleep Research*, 19, 207-213.

Salminen, S., Ruotsala, R., Vorne, J., & Saari, J. (2007). Työturvallisuuslain toimeenpano työpaikoilla. Selvitys uudistetun työturvallisuuslain vaikutuksista työpaikkojen turvallisuustoimintaan (Implementation of the Occupational Safety and Health Act at workplaces). Sosiaali- ja terveysministeriön selvityksiä 2007:4. Helsinki: Yliopistopaino. (in Finnish)

Salminen, S., & Saloniemi, A. (2010). Fixed-term work and violence at work. *International Journal of Occupational Safety and Ergonomics*, 16, 323-328.

Salminen, S., Vartia, M., & Giorgiani, T. (2009). Occupational injuries of immigrant and Finnish bus drivers. *Journal of Safety Research*, 40, 203-205.

Saloniemi, A., & Oksanen, H. (1998). Accidents and fatal accidents - some paradoxes. *Safety Science*, 29, 59-66.

Saloniemi, A., & Salminen, S. (2010). Do fixed-term workers have a higher injury rate? *Safety Science*, 48, 693-697.

Sinisalo, A. (2012). Expected injury cost indices on Finnish farms. *Journal of Agricultural Safety and Health*, 18, 31-43.

Sinks, T., Mathias, C. G. T., Halperin, W., Timbrook, C., & Newman, S. (1987). Surveillance of work-related cold injuries using Workers' Compensation claims. *Journal of Occupational Medicine*, 29, 504-509.

Statistics Finland. (2007). Tilastokatsaus 2007:1. Helsinki. (in Finnish)

Statistics Finland. (2010). Work force study 2009. www.stat.fi/til/2009/12/tyti_2009_12_2010-01-26_tie_001_fi.html. Retrieved 9.3.2012.

Statistics Finland. (2011a). Population at the end or 2010. www.stat.fi/tup/suoluk/suoluk_vaesto.html. Retrieved 8.3.2012.

Statistics Finland. (2011b). Accidents at Work 2009. www.stat.fi/til/ttap/2009/ttap_2009_2011-11-30_tie_001_fi.html. Retrieved 12.3.2012

Statistics Finland. (2011c). Itsemurhien määrä pienin yli 40 vuoteen (The number of suicides lowest during the period of over 40 years). www.stat.fi/til/ksyyt/2010/ksyyt_2010_2011-12-16_tie_011_f.html. Retrieved 11.4.2012.

Statistics Korea. (2011a). National land area in 2010. http://www.index.go.kr/egams/stts/jsp/potal/stts/PO_STTS_IdxMain.jsp?idx_cd=2728&bbs=INDX_001&clas_div=A (accessed on 13.3.2012) (in Korean)

Statistics Korea. (2011b). Population and population density by region in 2010. http://www.index.go.kr/egams/stts/jsp/potal/stts/PO_STTS_IdxMain.jsp?idx_cd=1007&bbs=INDX_001&clas_div=A (accessed on 13.3.2012) (in Korean)

Statistics Korea. (2011c). Employment trend in December 2011. http://kostat.go.kr/portal/korea/kor_nw/2/3/2/index.board (accessed on 4.4.2012). (in Korean)

Stuckler, D., Basu, S., Suhrcke, M., Coutts, A., & McKee, M. (2011). Effects of the 2008 recession on health: a first look at European data. *Lancet*, 378, 124-125.

Taattola, K., Rautiainen, R. H., Karttunen, J. P., Suutarinen, J., Viluksela, M. K., Louhelainen, K., & Mäittälä, J. (2012). Risk factors for occupational injuries among full-time farmers in Finland. *Journal of Agricultural Safety and Health*, 18, 83-93.

Targum, S. D., & Kitanaka, J. (2012). Overwork suicide in Japan: A national crisis. *Innovations in Clinical Neuroscience*, 9, 35-38.

Tynkkynen, M. (2012). Statutory accident insurance system in Finland. Helsinki: Federation of Accident Insurance Institutions.

Ulfberg, J., Carter, N., & Edling, C. (2000). Sleep-disordered breathing and occupational accidents. *Scandinavian Journal of Work, Environment & Health*, 26, 237-242.

Uusitalo, H., Ruotsala, R., & Niskanen, T. (2012). Asioita saatiin kuntoon. Työsuojelun valvontalain vaikutus työpaikkojen työsuojelutoimintaan (Things have been put in order. Effects of the occupational safety and health enforcement act on the workplace safety activities). Sosiaali- ja terveysministeriön julkaisuja 2011:18. Helsinki: Sosiaali- ja terveysministeriö. (in Finnish)

Vahtera, J., Pentti, J., Helenius, H., & Kivimäki, M. (2006). Sleep disturbances as a predictor of long-term increase in sickness absence among employees after family death or illness. *Sleep*, 29, 673-682.

Vegso, S., Cantley, L., Slade, M., Taiwo, O., Sircar, K., Rabinowitz, P., Fiellin, M., Russi, M. B., & Cullen, M. R. (2007). Extended work hours and risk of acute occupational injury: A case-crossover study of workers in manufacturing. *American Journal of Industrial Medicine*, 50, 597-603.

Viikari-Juntura, E., Kausto, J., Shiri, R., Kaila-Kangas, L., Takala, E.-P., Karppinen, J., Miranda, H., Luukkonen, R., & Martimo, K.-P. (2012). Return to work after early part-time sick leave due to musculoskeletal disorders: a randomized controlled trial. *Scandinavian Journal of Work, Environment & Health*, 38, 134-143.

Virtanen, M., Kivimäki, M., Joensuu, M., Virtanen, P., Elovainio, M., & Vahtera, J. (2005). Temporary employment and health: a review. *International Journal of Epidemiology*, 34, 610-622.

Wagstaff, A. S., & Sigstad Lie, J.-A. (2011). Shift and night work and long working hours - a systematic review of safety implications. *Scandinavian Journal of Work, Environment and Health*, 37, 173-185.

Wilkins, K., & Mackenzie, S. G. (2007). Work injuries. *Health Reports*, 18 (3), 1-18.

Wirtz, A., Lombardi, D. A., Willetts, J. L., Folkard, S. & Christiani, D. C. (2012). Gender differences in the effect of weekly working hours on occupational injury risk in the United States working population. *Scandinavian Journal of Work, Environment and Health* 38, 349-357.

Yoon, J. D. (2011). Industrial accident prevention system in Korea - An introductory guide. Seoul: Korea Labor Institute.

Yrjänheikki, E., & Savolainen, H. (2000). Occupational safety and health in Finland. *Journal of Safety Research*, 31, 177-183.

In: Occupational Safety and Health
Editors: I.G. Kavouras, M.C.G. Chalbot

ISBN: 978-1-63117-695-1
© 2014 Nova Science Publishers, Inc.

Chapter 6

DEVELOPMENTS REGARDING THE INTEGRATION OF THE OCCUPATIONAL SAFETY AND HEALTH WITH QUALITY AND ENVIRONMENT MANAGEMENT SYSTEMS

Gilberto Santos[1,2], *Manuel Rebelo*[2], *Síria Barros*[1], *Rui Silva*[2], *Martinha Pereira*[1], *Gabriela Ramos*[1] *and Nuno Lopes*[1]

[1]College of Technology - Polytechnic Institute Cavado e Ave, Barcelos, Portugal
[2]CLEGI – Lusíada University - V. N. Famalicão – Portugal

ABSTRACT

The purpose of this chapter is to characterize the developments of Portuguese Small and Medium Enterprises (SMEs) and view the Occupational Health and Safety Management Systems (OHSMS) certification process after receiving the Quality Management System (QMS) certification as well as the integration of management systems. References were based on the ISO 9001 standard for a Quality Management Systems (QMS) and OHSAS 18001 for OHSMS. The method used to evaluate the implemented systems was by questionnaire. The questionnaire was sent to 300 SMEs; 46 responses were received and validated. Of them, only 12 SMEs had the OHSMS certificate according to OHSAS 18001. Moreover, 34 SMEs did not have the OHSMS certificate. The questionnaire probed for the main reasons SMEs opted for non-certification. The driving reason was related to high costs, while the main reasons to gain certification were, among others, to eliminate or minimize risks to workers. The primary benefits that certification has provided to Portuguese SMEs include: improved working conditions, ensuring compliance with legislation, and better internal communication about risks and hazards.

A case study is also presented about the observed integration level of management systems, quality, environment, and safety in a specific Portuguese Company, considering the application of the Plan-Do-Check-Act-Improve cycle, the similarities between the several Management Systems Standards (MSS), and the compatibilities of the requirements which enhance the integration for Occupational Health and Safety (OHSAS 18001 at work, Environment (ISO 14001), and Quality (ISO 9001). Strategy and research methods were supported in an inductive approach in the context of the investigator's experiences with the object and the environment of the study. The technique used to evaluate contributions was the internal investigation by questionnaire to the collaborators of the company. The potential benefits of the observed integration are: the elimination of conflicts between individual systems with resource optimization; creation of added value to the business by eliminating several types of organizational wastes; and reducing the number of documented procedures, and other written documents and records.

INTRODUCTION

The OHSMS (Occupational Health and Safety Management System) certification liberates companies from direct public control, and can be regarded as a self-regulatory tool. Furthermore, in recent years, these systems have been improved and further developed. This development is consistent with the demand of external accountability in other areas, initially exemplified by the ISO 9001 quality standard developed in the early 1990s (Power, 2008). Certification of products and processes began during the 1960's in the manufacturing industry, as a tool to control and assure the quality/conformity of products and services provided by suppliers to customers/consumers (Wright, 2000). At first, the implementation of a Quality Management System (QMS) was particularly relevant in demanding, high activity sectors, like the automotive and aeronautical industries, but it has been rapidly extended to other activity sectors, becoming a common tool of many companies worldwide and a factor in competition and survival. The aim of QMS has been to reduce defective products and lost time, as well as to improve customer satisfaction and excellence. The second management system to be implemented and certified was the Environmental Management System (EMS). Due to increasing demands of environmental legislation in developed countries, many companies are now required to seriously consider not only environmental aspects associated to the production chain but also to the life cycle of their products. They are forced to implement suitable Environmental Management Systems (EMS) to reduce waste and to protect the environment. This is a particularly important issue for small and medium-sized companies (SMEs) that comprise the vast majority of business in Europe (Zorpas, 2010). Management Systems Standards (MSSs) have developed in an unprecedented manner in the last few years. The impact generated by quality, environmental, and other MSSs is demonstrated by the importance of such standards worldwide, ISO 9001 and ISO 14001. In particular, at the end of 2009, ISO 9001 accounted for 1,064,785 registered companies in more than 170 countries and ISO 14001 for 223,149 in about 150 countries. From 2006 to the end of 2009, the number of certifications had increased by 167,856 ISO 9001 certificates and 94,938 ISO 14001 certificates (Simon et al., 2012). On the other hand, according to Casadesús (2008), and other authors, the interest shown by organizations and other entities linked by the implementation of EMS, especially the family of ISO 14000 standards and the EMAS regulation in Europe, has grown exponentially all over the world in recent years, even though a certain saturation has been detected in some countries. Thus, the implementation and management of all economic, environmental and social aspects within a company is gradually becoming a crucial requirement for any business and has become a widespread phenomenon around the world (Zeng et al., 2007). Large companies are increasingly requiring this management policy from their suppliers, establishing specific requests and performances that SMEs often find extremely difficult to accomplish. On other hand, there are many organizations, which either because of the demands of the market itself or because of other internal motivations, have implemented different MSs alongside with their EMS. In fact, although no reliable references on this matter have been found, it is quite plausible to think that the great majority of ISO 14001 registered companies are also certified in accordance with the ISO 9001 standard (Karapetrovic and Casadesús, 2009). In most cases, the sequence of implementation will trail the publication of standards: ISO 9001-based QMS would be introduced first, followed by an ISO 14001- compliant

EMS (Karapetrovic and Casadesús, 2009). Thus, quality management philosophy and methods have been imported into ISO 14001 from ISO 9000. As a result, it is not surprising that measurement and evaluation are enshrined as important hallmarks of an effective EMS. Generally speaking, this component of the EMS is considered effective when the contents of review meetings are well communicated, the focus of meetings is on improving the system, findings (i.e., about noncompliance, from various statistical charts and audit results) are reported honestly, and corrective actions follow (Fryxell, 2002). In some cases, the similarities between QMS and EMS systems can facilitate the integration of the two related management systems (Tarí and Molina-Azorín, 2010). The people that work in environmental management and, at the same time, are members of quality teams assure that quality management goes hand-in-hand with environmental management.

On other hand, improved environmental management in the industrial sector is required to protect the environment, protect human health and property, and to satisfy environmental requirements associated with international trade (Kwon et al., 2002). Moreover, creating and maintaining a safe working environment ensures that workers have high health levels, protecting them from accidents, illness, or discomfort in the workplace and increases the efficiency of work processes, improves employee perceptions of their working environment, and leads to higher recruitment attractiveness (Tsai and Chou, 2009). Such aspects generate obvious benefits for entrepreneurs and employees, increasing a company's competitiveness while decreasing social costs. To achieve such a goal, companies are now implementing Occupational Health and Safety Management System (OHSMS), creating sustainable competitive advantages. The OHSMS provides a set of tools that enhances safety risk management efficiency related to all the organization's work activities. This system should be considered as part of the management system of any organization (Santos et al., 2008). Moreover, according to Granerud and Rocha (2011), the OHSMS is a systematic means for employers to handle challenges and reduce haphazard attitudes to risks and problems in the work environment. OHSMS certification makes it possible for firms to document a certain pattern of working conditions to demonstrate to both the public at large and its own customers that they are living up to established production standards. On the other hand, the OHSMS certification is a form of soft regulation requiring the company to fulfill certain legal obligations, as well as engage in organizational processes to promote the continuous improvement of health and safety conditions (Granerud and Rocha, 2011). The main reasons regarding the interest in a safety scheme by SMEs is the desire to improve or ensure the health and safety of employees, and to raise awareness across organization (Vassie and Cox, 1998). Analysis of one study's data revealed that employees in companies with OHSAS 18001, ISO 9001, and no certification at all, perceive safety variables from different perspectives (Vinodkumar and Bhasi, 2011). OHSAS 18001 certified organizations are significantly higher compared with the others. Additionally, regulations based on ISO 9000 have been created to guide companies in developing systems for management and prevention of worker risks. Annexes A and B of ISO 9001:2008 add various clauses and sub-clauses related to the necessary elements of this standard (Vinodkumar and Bhasi, 2011). Due to this, certified management systems are increasingly being used by enterprises to document and develop conformance in a variety of different areas. Thus, according to Fernández-Muñiz et al. (2007), several fields are showing increasing interest in safety culture as a means of reducing accidents in the workplace. Hence, the progressive implementation of ideas and techniques related to quality management is one of the clearest demonstrations of organizational innovation in the industry in the last few decades. From the standpoint of risk prevention literature, it has been argued that the use of advanced quality management systems has helped reduce accident rates, because quality management methods are based on the principle of prevention rather than corrective actions. Hence, the concept of an OHSMS has become common over the past 20 years (Robson et al., 2007).The actions that are carried out to achieve quality are the same actions necessary, for example, to achieve effective risk management (Herrero et al., 2002). In line with this, OHSAS 18001 has become compatible with the ISO 9001. This means that compliance requirements for OHSAS 18001 are similar to those for ISO 9001; though, the fact is that OHSAS 18001 is an occupational health and safety reference, whereas ISO 9001 is a quality management standard (Vinodkumar and Bhasi, 2011). Hence, if the aim of achieving quality is to remove deviations in the production process, it is clear that the occurrence of an accident is an unforeseen and undesirable situation. Thus, the implementation of quality control mechanisms is intended to reduce failures in the system, including workplace accidents (Arocena, 2008). If the aim of achieving quality is to remove deviations in the production process, then the implementation of quality control mechanisms can reduce failures in the system, including workplace accidents. On the other hand, if the history of quality management is analyzed, one can observe that the concept of quality evolves from quality control to quality assurance. In quality assurance, planning and company culture are directed with the client and end product in mind. In terms of safety, workers and managers of the company are the clients and safety is the product (absence of injuries and illnesses) (Roberge, 1999). In line with this, if the evolution of quality management is analyzed, the results should show that three stages exist: (a) quality control, (b) quality assurance, and (c) total quality. If the same analysis is carried out for the safety management system, three similar stages would be found: (a) safety control, (b) safety assurance or guarantee, and (c) total safety (Herrero et al., 2002). Considering increases in industrial accidents, loss of life, and material and environmental issues, more and more organizations are voluntarily embracing management system certifications. These management system certifications are expected to integrate safety management with the rest of the functions of the organization (Vinodkumar and Bhasi, 2011). Further, it would be expected that the joint use of advanced quality management techniques and innovative occupational risk prevention management would generate some synergetic effect in reducing occupational risk. However, companies need peaceful and healthy working environments that protect their assets from accidents, illnesses, or discomfort in the workplace. Choudhry et al. (2007) consider that an organization is a safety culture in which safety is regarded as being an issue that concerns everyone. As a result, safety rules should be understood and adhered to; all incidents must be reported and investigated quickly, appropriate actions must be determined and taken, and lessons pertaining to accident events must be learned. "Changing or new work environment" is a broad term covering new trends in work environments (Koukoulaki, 2010).

In the 1980s, researchers suggested that the increasing importance of small enterprises indicated the beginning of a new era for industrial production in which the industry would break away from the dehumanizing effects of Fordism and Taylorism (Piore and Sabel, 1984). On other hand, the majority of studies find that small enterprises have a greater accident risk as compared to large enterprises (Sørensen et al., 2007). According to González (2012), the future workplace will be composed of micro-enterprises, flexible and resilient. And according to the European Agency for Safety and Health at Work (2002), "Changing Work World" issues can be summarized as new work organizational forms, new contractual relationships, use of work time, new technologies, changes to the workforce, and changes in occupational health and safety systems.

Thus, Santos (2002) argues that human resources are the most valuable resource of any company or country, but not always the most valued by some leaders. Thus, the greatest asset of any organization, any region, or any country, is people with their know-how. In line with this, and according to Shapiro (2008), today *"almost two thirds of the value of a large company comes from intangible assets - what they know and the ideas and relationships that have: patents and copyrights, the databases and the brand, organizational arrangements and training or human capital to use these ideas"*. Thus, trained and experienced workers who die or become injured result in disruptions to work progress and, undeniably, represent a reduction in construction, or industry performance. Nonetheless, difficulties may arise when researchers use different techniques to measure safety performance. Traditional measures of safety performance rely on some form of accident or injury data.

The literature show that safety culture is a multidimensional concept that now identifies companies that desire greater profitability and better organization implementation of the QMS, followed by EMS and OHSMS. The certification of such Management Systems requires accomplishing specific standards (ISO 9001 standards for QMS, ISO 14001 standards for EMS, and OHSAS 18001 standards for OHSMS (Santos et al., 2012) and submitting the organization to periodical audits. Nevertheless, the implementation and management of these three systems, in parallel, requires many duplicate management tasks and different human resources, making it difficult to implement and ensure their alignment with the organization's strategy (Zeng et al., 2007). These three standards contain the same basic principles and a general common structure (Fresner and Engelhardt, 2004; Block and Marash, 2002). They all require the definition of roles and responsibilities, the training personnel, the definition of written procedures, controlling and keeping records of documentation and data, continuously improving by applying "root cause" analysis to corrective and preventive action, performing internal audits, and so on (Wright, 2000; Zeng et al., 2007). Thus, it may be of great benefit to integrate them, which can be done at different levels (Jørgensen et al., 2006). On other hand, according to the ISO – IMS publication (The integrated use of management systems standards) (ISO, 2008), a common objective of management system standards is to assist organizations to manage the risks associated with providing products and services to customers and other stakeholders.

On other hand, the management systems of many organizations are frequently split into a number of parts or sub-systems, which must be managed separately with relative independence. These parts or sub-systems of an organization's management system reflect the different needs and expectations of the stakeholders. Many organizations use standards, such as those related to quality, the environment, and safety, among others, to manage certain aspects of their performance (Rebelo, 2011). The following questions may arise: How can these three management systems be integrated? In recent years, the standards for management systems have become more compatible, and organizations may need support to understand the common principles and approaches to Integrated Management Systems (IMS). The number of companies with more than one certification is rising steadily, and many of them are already experimenting with integration. According to Rasmussen (2007), there is no one single international standard for IMS. For this reason, several countries, such as England, New Zealand, Australia, France, the Netherlands, Denmark and Spain, have developed or are developing their own IMS standard" (Jørgensen et al., 2006; Salomone, 2008). The PAS 99:2012 (England), the DS 8001:2005 (Denmark), and the UNE 66177:2005 (Spain) standards tackle the issue of integration and emphasize the importance of the Deming's Cycle - PDCA; they are based on the model of processes, with focus on the business strategy and on the expectations of the stakeholders. They also suggest other approaches and possible integration methods. The obvious first steps towards the definition of an IMS are: increasing the compatibility between the standards, identifying cross-references, and ensuring proper internal coordination of the elements in the Management System (Jørgensen et al., 2006).

Thus, management systems integration is a step forward, and standard ISO 19011 (to guide management systems audits combined) is a good example of that. Moreover, a single integrated management system is coordinated by a multidisciplinary team, thereby saving both financial and human resources which is a key issue for the future (Santos et al., 2013; Mendes and Santos, 2009). Combining all three Management Systems in order to implement a single IMS is considered to promote significant cost reduction (in external audits, for example) which will depend on the size of the organization and the nature of its activity (Wright, 2000). Moreover, integration is considered to have a *beneficial effect on the culture of the organization, in that it promotes less departmental 'isolation ', and more of a team ethic between the various functions* (Wright, 2000). A changing culture is dawning, one that is paving the way from *Total Quality* (TQ) to *Integrated Total Quality* (ITQ). When it is observed that there exists similar procedures in the referred standards, those are adapted to the two or more systems and jointly audited. However, the manuals remain, still, individually separated. As stated by Santos *et al.* (2013), although an audit may be integrated/joint (combined audit), the respective reports are often kept separate, so that any nonconformities detected in one of the systems does not negatively affect any other management system that complies with the respective standard which could cause the loss of clients, which would be a drawback for the company and is considered one of the obstacles to quicker integration. Suditu (2007) associates the integration of management systems to internal motivations and corresponding benefits by dividing them into: 1 - Organizational – improvement of the quality of management by combining three departments into one and reducing barriers between individual systems; 2 - Financial – reduction in auditing costs; 3- Employees – increased motivation, awareness, and competencies; 4 - External motivations and corresponding benefits, by dividing them into commercial (competitive advantage, improved market position, increasing client base, and satisfying current client), communication (improved image of the organization, improved relationships with Stakeholders, and evidence of legal compliance). In fact, significant differences in these areas have not been found, and it is fairly plausible that the vast majority of companies certified under ISO 14001 are also certified under the ISO 9001 standard (Santos et al., 2011). Therefore, a new necessity has emerged in organizations, namely to integrate these systems into a single IMS and we cannot forget the fact that the environmental improvement of the product must be considered in relation to the impacts on Quality & Health and Safety (Jørgensen, 2008). Therefore, the idea of an IMS consists of establishing correspondences and to combine two or more independent management systems, for example: integrating ISO 9001, ISO 14001, and OHSAS 18001. Evidence of this can be seen in table A.1 - of the annex A - of OHSAS 18001:2007.

Despite having their origins in different areas within organizational structure, Quality, Environment, and Safety Management Systems have a lot in common (Fresner and Engelhardt, 2004; Block and Marash, 2002) in agreement with the ISO 72:2001 Guide. There are a number of common elements that can be arranged under the following main subjects: policy; planning; implementation and operation; performance assessment; improvement and management review (Santos et al., 2011). The integration of these management systems is attainable. The ISO 19011 standard - Guidelines for auditing management systems is a good example. The future lies in the integration of these and others management systems, managed by only one multidisciplinary team with training and skills in several areas, thereby economizing both financial and human resources (Santos et al., 2011).

A good example of Management Systems Certification and Integration in Portugal is represented in Figure 1. For a long time, the only foundry in the country to have its Quality, Environment, and Health and Safety systems certified was Kupper and Schmidt, a SME that supplies, exclusively, to the automotive industry and exports about 98% of its production to European and American markets.

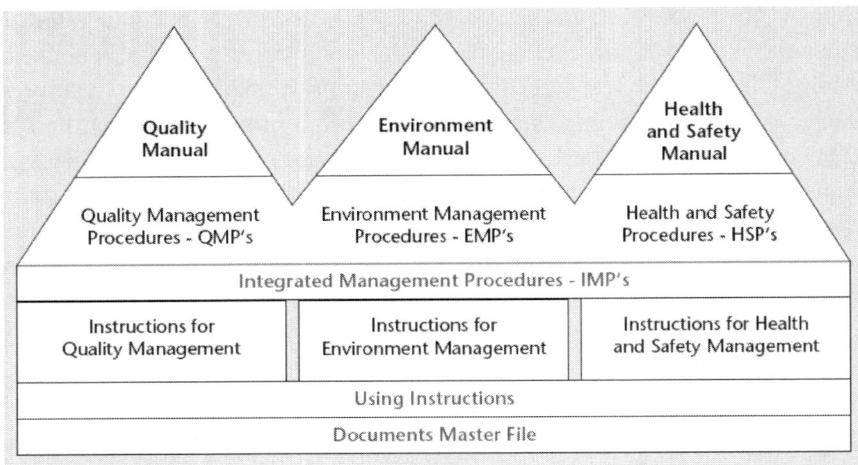

Figure 1. Documental structure of the Integrated Management Systems at Kupper & Schmidt. (Santos, 2011).

Just a few years after starting its activity, the company had its Quality System certified by its main customers. In 1997, it was certified according to ISO 9002 standard; in 1998, by QS – 9000; in 1999, by VDA 6.1; and in 2001, by ISO/TS 16949 standards. In 2000, the company focused on the environment and obtained certification according to the ISO 14001 standard. Since 2002, the company has had its Health and Safety System certified according to OHSAS 18001 (Santos et al., 2011). Presently, the company runs an IMS regarding management procedures, operating instructions, and documentation. The objective of this chapter is to characterize the development of Portuguese SMEs in the area of OHSMS, identify the reasons for certification, identify the difficulties associated with the OHSAS 18001 certification process, and discuss the primary benefits that arise from this certification in SMEs due to ISO 9001 QMS certification. Finally, a case study is presented regarding the development of the integration of the OHSMS with other systems, namely Quality Management Systems and Environment Management Systems.

METHODOLOGY

In recent years, there has been an increase in the number of quality certified companies and, also, a smaller increase in safety certifications. As a result, an investigation was undertaken concerning the importance of implementing these systems in Portuguese SMEs. A questionnaire was the instrument used to survey several Portuguese SMEs. This enabled a large amount of information to be collected economically, despite the high failure risk of many similar initiatives. Upon receipt of the completed questionnaires, the same were validated, as recommended by literature specific to the area, through a pre-test (Mendes, 2007). Twelve companies were involved. They represented various sectors of activity with at least one certification system implemented. The questionnaire was sent via e-mail or personal delivery.

The questionnaire was organized into various sections: 1- General Description of the Company; 2 - Quality System; 3- Safety System; 4- General Questions. The questionnaire looked at two main areas: a) reasons for certification and b) benefits gained from certification. A Likert scale was used (1 through 4) to allow each subject to assign a value indicating the magnitude of agreement to each item. Due to the questionnaire's structure, the system manager (subject) would be required to first assess the company's certified management system. They must make a quantitative analysis of the benefits, importance, and impact, mainly of the QMS and OHSMS. Inherent arguments were also identified, regarding the implementation of certification management systems.

After the questionnaire was approved, it was sent to SMEs via e-mail with the collaboration of the "Portuguese SMEs Association – Associação PME Portugal". Addresses were collected from the "Portuguese SMEs Association Database." The list of companies with quality certifications were collected from Business Association –Portugal's site (Associação Empresarial de Portugal). This sample is comprised of a heterogeneous group of industry, it includes the founding year and the number of employees. The final questionnaire was organized according to Table 1. Both qualitative and quantitative answers were asked, which depended on the question's nature and the available data.

The questionnaire was sent to 300 SMEs that are QMS certified. The survey was carried out via e-mail, accompanied by a cover letter which indicated the goals of the investigation. About 80 questionnaires were received. The main criteria for validation were: be a SME; have the ISO 9001 QMS certification; and, have answered the main questions completely. Only 46 were completed properly. Data was analyzed and the results were presented (Mendes, 2007); however, it is known that there are SMEs with other certified systems, among them the OHSMS. 12 of the 46 SMEs had OHSAS 18001 certification. Additionally, the questionnaire inquired about the main reasons for non-certification. The main reasons for no OHSAS 18001 certification are presented below.

**Table 1. Main sections and topics of the questionnaire
(Adapted from Santos et al., 2012)**

Main Sections	Questionnaire main topics
General Description of the Company	Number of employees; Volume of business; Branch of activity; Main products and markets; etc.
Quality Management System	Year of ISO 9001 certification; Main reasons for Quality Management System certification; Main difficulties; Main benefits that arose from certification (new costumers, image, competitiveness, business increase, quality improvement, customer satisfaction, products innovation, organization improvements, etc.); Main drawbacks; Quality tools that the company uses;
Occupational, Health and Safety Management System	Year of Occupational Health and Safety Management Systems certification according OHSAS 18001; Main reasons for Occupational Health and Safety Management Systems certification; Main difficulties; Main benefits that arose from certification, among others: ensuring compliance with legislation; number of accidents at work; costs of accidents and occupational diseases; absenteeism; number of employee suggestions; to fortify the image of the organization; risks of accidents, through the prevention of occupational risks; internal communication for workers about risks and hazardous. Main drawbacks;

All the SMEs that cooperated with this investigation had QMS certification but belonged to different types of industry. Within the 12 companies that participated, 58.3% (7 SMEs) were from the industrial sector, 25% (3) belonged to the electric/telecommunications sector, and 16.6% (2 SMEs) were from the trade/services sector. Although many SMEs connected to the building sector have the Portuguese Standard NP 4397:2008 OHSMS certifications, it was reported that they still had a long way to go. The construction industry is one of the sectors with the highest death rates in

Portugal. Thus, a detailed statistical response analysis was not carried out. This study presents the benefits, drawbacks, and difficulties concerning the OHSMS certification process.

Survey data recorded in an Excel spreadsheet was exported to SPSS (Statistical Package for Social Sciences). SPSS is powerful statistics software that provides the user with complex statistical calculations. However, two obstacles arose: 1) the small sample size and 2) knowing what statistical test to use, and (3) how to interpret the results correctly. Appropriate statistical techniques were used to analyze the data. Average, frequency plots, principal component analysis, cluster analysis and statistical inference were used to find important conclusions about the population, bearing in mind that small sample size is a limitation. The Kaiser-Meyer-Olkin (KMO) test and Bartlett's sphericity test were used to measure the quality of the correlation between variables. The KMO is a test that produces results that vary from 0 to 1 and compares zero-order correlations with the partial correlations observed between the variables.

Cronbach's Alpha was used as an estimate of *reliability*. It is commonly used to measure internal consistency of a group of variables (items). It can be defined as the correlation that is expected between the scale and other scales using the same hypothetical universe with an equal number of items that measure the same characteristic.

Cluster analysis was used as an exploratory technique. It is a type of multivariate analysis that groups variables into homogeneous groups or groups with common characteristics. Each observation belonging to a particular cluster is similar to all others belonging to that cluster and is different from the observations belonging to other clusters. The analysis of the survey was directed to the most relevant items of the questionnaire. Regarding OHSMS certification, for example, there were 14 items that corresponded to the items outlined in figure 2.

On other hand, it is also presented a case study concerning the integration of various systems, of which highlights, Occupational Health and Safety Management System according OHSAS 18001, Quality Management Systems according ISO 9001 and Environmental Management Systems according ISO 14001 that ran in one Portuguese company. A questionnaire was drafted, tested, validated, and distributed to a sample of collaborators from different departments of the company. The final questionnaire was organized into four sections, according to Table 2. One hundred and sixty employees integrated within the organizational structure of the company were surveyed. The rate of response was equal to 86%.

Table 2. Main sections and main topics of the questionnaire (Rebelo, 2011)

Main Sections	Questionnaire main topics
1 - Importance of motivation factors for the implementation of the IMS_QES.	• Improving the image of the company • Rationalizing and optimizing the management of the resources (financial, material and human) • Facilitating the management of the three components for the sustainable development of the organization and of the business • Increasing requirements of the costumers • Competitive advantage and strategic vision of the business • Natural evolution of the Management Systems in the company • The continual improvement of Quality, Environment and Safety Management Systems involves their integration
2 - Stakeholder influences on the performance and evolution of an IMS-QES	• Management Group - Orientations and evolution of QES and Sustainability policies • Customers, competitors, insurance companies, suppliers and official QES entities • Financial institutions • Local Management group and collaborators
3 - Main Internal difficulties for the development of the IMS-QES model and its implementation	• Deficit of human and material resources due to the strongly competitive environment and costs reduction; • Resistance to change • Diversity of products and services vis-a-vis customer's requirements and legal and other requirements • Do not explicitly fit in the objectives and priorities of the company • Lack of internal competences in Integration Management Systems • Do not exist an international standard for the integration of Management Systems
4 - Potential benefits resulting from the implementation of the IMS-QES	• Elimination of conflicts between individual management systems, and consequent resource optimization, namely human resources • Elimination of several organizational waste including at the level of bureaucracy associated to the sub systems Quality, Environment and Safety • Common management policy, objectives, goals and KPIs - Key Process Indicators related to QES performance • Better and greater visibility of operation of the organization in the areas concerned • Improvement of the internal and external image of the company in the aim of the QES issues • Involvement and consolidation, by all employees, of a continual improvement culture, attitudes and values of global QES scope • Reduction of the number of internal and/or external audits and to suppliers • Improvement at the level of coordinated and integrated management of the Risk associated to the Safety of people, infrastructures, environment, and products • Greater employee valorization and motivation • Integrated management of several components of Sustainability in a Global Market; • Improvement of the partnership relationships with suppliers of goods and services;

The sample was identified by using as a reference the organizational structure of the company at the date of the survey. After the questionnaire had been tested and improved, it was sent by e-mail to each one of the company employees in the sample, carefully selected according to their position in the hierarchy. The departments surveyed included: General Management; Human Resources; Finance; QHSE; IT; Operations and Marketing; and, Sales. Selection was made based upon the employee's potential for knowledge about the company and, particularly, at the level of the subjects under investigation. The sample that was considered - 49 employees, represents 30.62% of the total surveyed. 42 subjects answered the questionnaire. The response rate was 85.71%. This rate indicates a strong level of cooperation at all hierarchical levels of the organization, to complete the questionnaire. This, in itself, revealed a high level of interest among all company participants, with strong cooperation by management areas for the matters under investigation/ assessment. It was observed the integration level of the systems.

SURVEY RESULTS

The first system that was certified in Portuguese SMEs was the QMS. After this system was consolidated, the certified EMS followed. In some cases, the OHSMS was the last to be analyzed. This has been more or less the general rule that Portuguese SMEs have adopted when researching the number of certifications, where quality (QMS) stands out in first place, followed by the environmental certification (EMS) and finally the OHSMS certification. Hence, this chapter presents the results of OHSMS certification, after the QMS certification, as well as, the integration of the referred systems.

Occupational Health and Safety Management System (OHSMS)

Utilizing responses from the survey, the OHSMS was analyzed in each organization. Of the 46 SMEs participating in the survey, 26 % are certified by the same OHSMS. The number of companies with the OHSMS certificate in Portugal is very small, but it is gradually growing. Therefore, the interest was to study the degree of importance organizations place upon implementing and certifying the OHSMS in their organization. Table 3 displays the groups and includes the reasons that led to the implementation of the OHSMS in SMEs for the referred group.

**Table 3. Main reasons that led to the implementation of OHSMS
in accordance with OHSAS 18001 (Santos et al., 2012)**

Groups	Reasons that led to the implementation and certification of the OHSMS	Most Important	Important	Less Important
1-Valuing human capital	Eliminate or minimize risks to workers.	83.4%	0%	0%
2 – Business reason	Improvement of the organization image with the reduction of accidents at work.	8.3%	91.7%	8.3 %
3–Social Reason	High rate of absenteeism due to occupational diseases.	8.3%	0%	33.3 %
	Serious accidents at work.	0%	8.3%	33.3 %
	Rate of industrial accidents high.	0%	0%	25,1 %

According to Table 3, five variables were divided into three groups. Group 1 – "Valuing human capital" which enables maximum safety within an organization. The aim is to minimize or eliminate occupational accidents and diseases acquired in the workplace. This is the most important reason that led to the implementation of the OHSMS in SMEs, with 83.4% of the responses as "very important." It may be noted that the 12 companies with certified OHSMS are almost unanimous in the same issue by stating that this issue is very important. **Group 2** – "Business reason" in which the aim is to strengthen the organization's public image by reducing accidents to its workers and society. The majority of responses were "important." The SMEs chosen as the most accurate claimed they wanted "Improvement of the organization's image by reducing accidents" (91.7%). **Group 3** – "Social Reason" had 3 questions where the company goal is to minimize social problems, such as: "high rate of absenteeism due to occupational diseases," "serious accidents at work," and "rate of industrial accidents." All these items were considered less important, since questions were geared to "eliminate or minimize risks to workers." To reduce the related variables, cluster analysis was the method used due to the small sample size.

The Main Benefits Gained from the OHSMS Certification

According to Santos et al. (2012), the potential benefits associated with OHSMS can be more effectively summarized through a detailed analysis of their impact on Portuguese SMEs. Some of the companies that participated in this study received OHSMS certification very recently. As such, benefits were not yet apparent. However, all 12 OHSMS certified SMEs participated in answering these questions.

Cluster analysis separates the results of the certification into four groups according to their similarities. Thus, fourteen variables were divided into four groups. **Group 1-** System OHSMS, assesses the risks. It strengthens the image of the company for its employees and consumers, providing a safe and stable work environment. The topics of the questions were: *Improvement of the company's image in the market and community; Number of employee suggestions; and finally, Risks of occupational diseases.* **Group 2-** Improving safety culture in the company. It reduces risk and improves the image and relationship between employees. The topics of the questions were: *Improvement of working conditions; Ensuring compliance with legislation; Fortifying the organization's image; Notice to workers about the risks and dangers; and Risks of accidents through the prevention of occupational risks.* **Group 3-** Linked the performance of the OHSMS: how it controlled the number of accidents, absenteeism, increased employee motivation, and the cost of accidents and occupational diseases. The topics of the questions were: *The number of accidents at work; The reduction of accidents and occupational diseases costs; Absenteeism; Employee motivation.* **Group 4** demonstrated the image of the organization, i.e., public awareness of social responsibility. The topics of the questions were: *Number of cases of occupational diseases; and Advertisements in newspapers, TV, and internet of the public data of the occupational health and safety (OHS).*

Analysis of the chart (figure 2) shows the greatest impact (above 65% of responses) and main benefits these companies had gained from OHSMS certification: "Improvement of working conditions" clearly was the preferred response (91.6%).

In this response, SMEs were almost unanimous, responding that the working conditions were really improved with the implementation and certification of the OHSMS; another important response with great import was "Ensuring compliance with legislation" with 83.3% of responses. Legislation exists in order to be followed. Most Portuguese SMEs with certified OHSMS fulfill legal requirements. "Notice to workers about the risks and dangers at work" had a 75% positive response. Hence, it can be inferred that there may be "better internal communication for workers about risks and hazards" when an OHSMS is implemented.

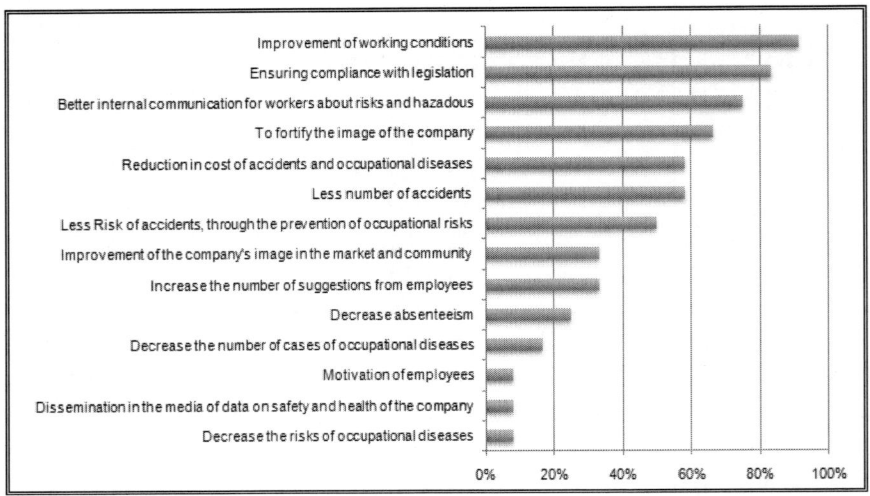

Figure 2. Distribution of main benefits companies obtained from OHSMS certification (Santos et al., 2012).

Less than 65%, but above 40%, of responses related to issues that had some impact on the companies; as such, they can be considered secondary benefits. Improving and fortifying the organization's image was believed to improve working conditions. Compliance with legislation results in better internal communication for workers which surely decreases the number of work related accidents (58.3%), reduces the cost of accidents and occupational diseases (58.3) and decreases accident risk through the prevention of occupational risks (50%).

In Table 4, there is a summary of the reasons for certification, as well as the main benefits and difficulties of the OHSMS certification. An important reason given for becoming certified was to "Eliminate or minimize risks to workers." Also presented are the benefits that had a major impact, such as: "Improvement of working conditions" and "Ensuring compliance with legislation". No drawbacks were given by the subjects. Inferred from the questionnaire, 100% of the companies with QMS and OHSMS certifications had a system of medicine in place at work. It appears that 82% of QMS and OHSMS SMEs had a procedure they used for making a systematic assessment of the risks of accidents. Regarding activities aimed at improving working conditions and preventing occupational diseases, 80% of companies with two certified management systems were implementing these activities through training and raising awareness. But for enterprises with only the QMS certificate, just 40% of SMEs had activities aimed at improving work conditions and the prevention of diseases. Whereas, 100% of the companies with two certified management systems were implementing the use of personal protective equipment at the time of the survey.

Table 4. Summary of the reasons for certification, as well, the benefits and difficulties that companies obtained with certification of the OHSMS. (Adapted from Santos et al., 2012)

OHSMS			100% are certified by ISO 9001; 26.09 % are certified by OHSAS 18001	
	Reasons for certification	Very important	Eliminate or minimize risks to workers	
		Important	Improving the organization image with the reduction of accidents at work	
		Less Important	Rate of absenteeism due to occupational diseases	
			Low serious accidents at work	Rate of industrial minor accidents high
	Benefits	Major Impact	Improvement of working conditions	Better internal communication for workers about risks and hazardous.
			Improvement company image.	Ensuring compliance with legislation
		Impact	Less number of accidents	Reduction in cost of accidents and occupational diseases
			Less Risk of accidents, occupational risks	through the prevention of
			Decrease absenteeism	Decrease the number of cases of occupational diseases
		Little Impact	Increase the number of suggestions from employees	Improvement of the company's image in the market and community
			Decrease the risks of occupational diseases	Motivation of employees
		No impact	Dissemination in the media of data on safety and health of the company	
	Drawbacks		No drawbacks have been referred	
	Main Difficulties		High certification costs	Difficulties to change Company's culture
			Difficulties to motivate personal	Increase bureaucracy
			Management difficulties in the early stages of certification	

The Main Benefits Gained from the IMS - QES Integration

The emphasis placed by the respondents of the case study, both for the present and fundamentally for the future, on the range of potential benefits identified and evaluated as being the result of the implementation of an IMS-QES, in itself, particularly justifies and validates the implementation of such a system and makes it an enormous priority.

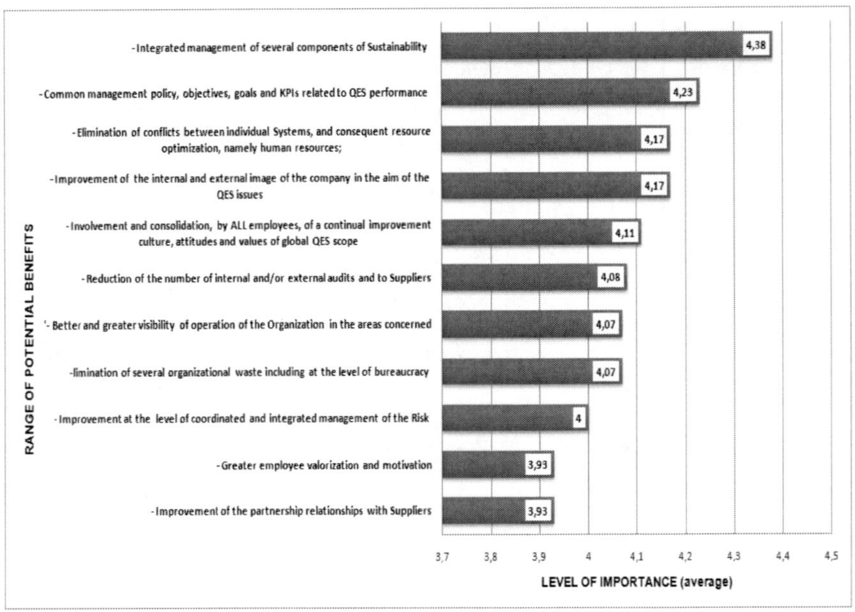

Figure 3. Main benefits resulting from the implementation of an IMS-QES (Rebelo, 2011).

Figure 3 illustrates some of the benefits given by the subjects of our study: the elimination of conflicts between individual systems and the optimization of resources, specifically human resources related to management and operationalization; the integrated management of sustainability components in a global market, where quality no longer makes a competitive difference and is now just a starting point for a business; the improvement of partnerships with suppliers of goods and services; dialogue with our main stakeholders and commitment to their ongoing satisfaction and increased contribution to the company's competitiveness; common management policy, objectives, targets and KPIs (Key Process Indicators) related to QES performance; the creation of added value for the business through the elimination of waste, especially that of bureaucracy associated with independent management systems and their certifications, including the laboratories and MID (Module D); improvement to the company's internal and external image and to its credibility in QES areas, specifically in relationships with clients, official entities and other stakeholders; improvements to the coordinated and integrated management of risks to the safety of people and property, the environment, and the quality of products from "cradle to grave"; a reduction in the number of internal and/or external audits and audits of suppliers and the consequent amount of time taken and associated costs; greater valuation and motivation of employees as a result of the expansion of their skill base, actions and responsibilities, with their resulting empowerment; and the integrated management of sustainability components.

Similarities between the Management System Standards Which Enhance the Integration - Matrix tf Compatibility of the Requirements and of Support to hhe Integration

The ISO defines as principles of Quality Management: customer focus; leadership; involvement of people; process approach; system approach to management; continual improvement; factual approach to decision making; and mutually beneficial supplier relationships. According to the ISO Guide 72:2001, anyone drafting these and other management standards must take into account that the corresponding management systems must consider the following phases of the PDCAI cycle (Plan, Do, Check, Act and Improve): policies and principles; planning; implementation, and operation ; performance assessment; improvement; and management review. Within this framework, taking into account the structuring of standards pertaining to management responsibility/planning, resource management, product realization/operational control, measurement, analysis, and improvement on the matrix of the table 3, we have shown the requirements of the ISO 9001, ISO 14001, and OHSAS 18001, as well as having established correspondences, made them compatible with each other and associated with the phases of the PDCAI cycle. With this matrix, we aim to orient and align the organizational structure of the company, while at the same time creating a structured and useful reference to inform effective alignment and connect the Sub-Management Systems of Quality, Environment and Safety with consequent compatibilities for consequent implementation of the IMS-QES. From this matrix, we can also, at the same time, make connections with the Deming Cycle, in this circumstance for the Integrated Management System as well as a set of steps (1.1; 2.1...2.4; 3.1...3.7; 4.1...4.6 and 5.1) associated with the PDCAI cycle.

From Individual Systems to Integration - Observed Integration Level

At this point, a reference to the company's organizational and operational structure of observed integration level, which in an organizational context by business lines (energy and water) of the International Group to which it belongs, includes a management area (the management of Quality, Environment and Safety (QES). The manager, within the scope of his job description, responsibility, and authority, ensures at all levels of the company the coordination of the QES and Laboratory Management Systems. The manager ensures also, its development and planning and that the decisions that are approved by Top Management concerning consequences and cooperation with the strategy and policies of the development of the QES inside the International Group in which the company are integrated.

The organizational structure of the QES Management includes a group of functional and operational areas whose managers have responsibility for and authority over ensuring that the requirements of each sub-system, either operated in an isolated way or in inter-action with others, are understood by all employees and implemented at the company, in a coherent manner as established.

It has been observed across companies that there exists an integrated QES management policy. This policy figures in the Quality Manual, in the Environmental Management Manual, and in the Occupational Health and Safety Manual and establishes coherent and defining principles and proposals for common actions and responsibilities for the Integrated Management of Quality, the Environmental and Occupational Health, & Safety issues. Similarly, it states that the main purpose of all work done by all employees is the continuous improvement of their performance in the areas of Quality, the protection and promotion of the Environment, Occupational Health, and the Safety of the Employees and Company's property, with the aim of its sustainable success.

Table 5. Matrix of compatibility of the standards requirements and of support to the integration of the Sub-systems (Rebelo, 2011)

PHASE I - PLAN

1 - INTEGRATED MANAGEMENT POLICY	ISO 9001	ISO 14001	OHSAS 18001
1.1 - Management commitment / Continuous improvement	5.1 5.3 8.5.1	4.2	4.2
2 - PLANNING			
2.1- Identification of : product requirements, aspects, impacts, hazards and risks and their assessment	5.2 7.2.1 7.2.2	4.3.1	4.3.1
2.2 - Identification, access to and updating of legal requirements and other requirements of Stakeholders	5.2 7.2.1 7.2.2	4.3.2	4.3.2

PHASE II - DO

3 - IMPLEMENTATION AND OPERATION	ISO 9001	ISO 14001	OHSAS 18001
3.1 - Resources, organizational structure, roles, responsibilities and authority	5.1 5.5.1 5.5.2 6.1 6.3	4.4.1	4.4.1
3.2 - Training, awareness, competence and qualifications	6.2.1 6.2.2	4.4.2	4.4.2
3.3 - Communication, participation and consultation of the Stakeholders	5.5.3 7.2.3	4.4.3	4.4.3
3.4 - QES Management System documentation	4.2.1	4.4.4	4.4.4

PHASE III - CHECK

4 - CHECKING AND CORRECTION	ISO 9001	ISO 14001	OHSAS 18001
4.1 - Performance monitoring and measurement of processes and products	7.6 8.1 8.2.3 8.2.4 8.4	4.5.1	4.5.1
4.2 - Evaluation of compliance	8.2.3 8.2.4	4.5.2	4.5.2
4.3 - Incident investigation	---	---	4.5.3.1
4.4 - Non-conformities; corrections; corrective and preventive actions / Control of nonconforming products	8.3 8.4 8.5.2 8.5.3	4.5.3	4.5.3.2

Table 5. (Continued)

	ISO 9001	ISO 14001	OHSAS 18001
2.3 -Definition of objectives, targets and Programmesof QES management and improvement	5.4.1 5.4.2 8.5.1	4.3.3	4.3.3
2.4 - Definition of the plans of response to emergency situations	8.3	4.4.7	4.4.7

	ISO 9001	ISO 14001	OHSAS 18001
3.5 - Control of documents	4.2.3	4.4.5	4.4.5
3.6 - Product realization Operational control	7.1 to 7.5.5	4.4.6	4.4.6
3.7 - Operationalisation of contingency plans.	8.3	4.4.7	4.4.7

PHASE IV - ACT

	ISO 9001	ISO 14001	OHSAS 18001
4.5 - Records Control	4.2.4	4.5.4	4.5.4
4.6 - Combined Internal QES Audits	8.2.2	4.5.5	4.5.5
5 - MANAGEMENT REVIEW			
5.1 - Critical analysis and combined QES Management System review	5.1 5.6.1 5.6.2 5.6.3 8.5.1	4.6	4.6

CONTINUAL IMPROVEMENT OF THE IMS_QES

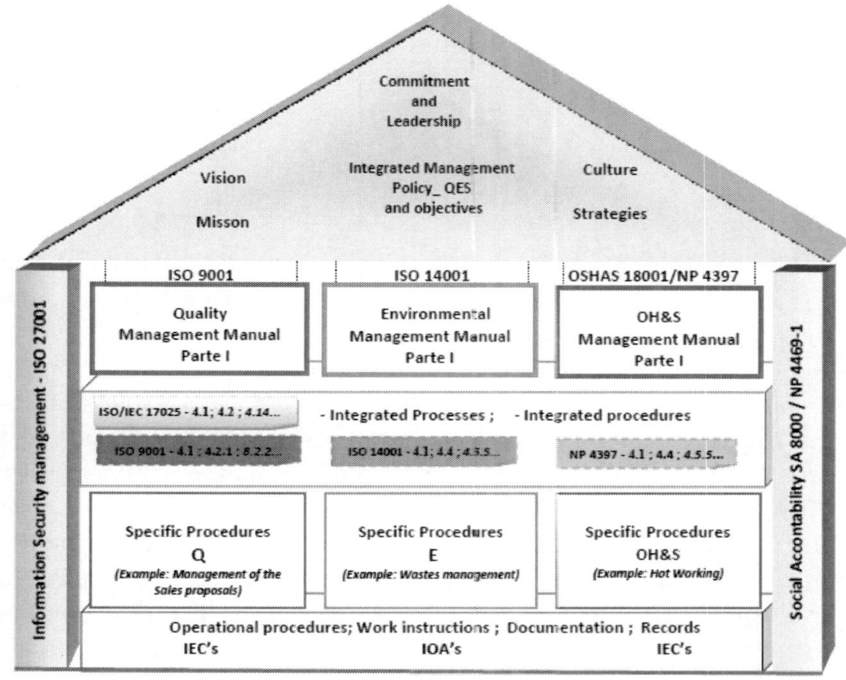

Figure 4. From individual systems to integration - observed integration level in the company (Rebelo, 2011).

Evolution in the company and observed integration levels can also be seen in documentation, in the context of this chapter, which has led to the creation of some documented processes and procedures that are common to the three QES Management Systems and accredited Laboratories and which are also aimed at meeting the requirements of other standards. Examples of this are the processes control plan and some documentation procedures. In turn, there is a single annual program of combined internal QES audits and audits to suppliers, which is operated under the responsibility of a team of internal auditors qualified to perform combined QES audits as per the following standards: ISO 9001, ISO 14001, OHSAS 18001, and ISO/IEC 1702. The realization of combined audits by a third party (by the certification body) within the scope of QMS, EMS, and MID includes the simultaneous management review of the QES management systems, the definition of management indicators and processes that are common to the three individual QES Management systems and their mapping on a integrated process map, as well as, the KPIs. These are important components of management characterized by integration, which were observed in the company, schematically shown in fig. 4, as a result of recent natural evolution, that will illustrate the final step of the structure.

DISCUSSION

Among others, the main benefits and consequent developments that Portuguese SMEs have gained from being certified by the OHSMS, according to OHSAS 18001, were: 1- Improvement of conditions in the workplace; 2 - Ensuring compliance of safety and health legislation; 3 - Better internal communication for workers about risks and hazardous; and 4 - Solidifying the company's image. In relation to the improvement of health and safety conditions in the workplace, this research is in line with the study done by Tsai and Chou (2009). Tsai and Chou stated that creating and maintaining a safe working environment assures the workers improved health levels, protects them from accidents, illness, or discomfort in the workplace, and increases the efficiency of work processes as well as employee's perceptions of the working environment. Along the same lines, Mossink (2002) claimed that satisfactory working conditions provide benefits of many kinds, and the beneficiaries are both direct and indirect participants. Direct beneficiaries are the workers themselves, since they are those most affected by accidents, although the firm also benefits, because it avoids losses and improves profitability. Indirect beneficiaries are the insurers, contractors, consumers, families, and society in general. Nowadays, there is wide recognition in professional literature regarding views on safety culture as an essential element in the organization's efforts to prevent accidents in the workplace (Fernández-Muñiz et al., 2007). Moreover, technological progress and intense competitive pressures bring rapid change in working conditions, work processes, and organization. Legislation is often insufficient in addressing those changes completely or keeping pace with new hazards and risks (Bottani et al., 2009). This study uncovered the need to comply with legislation even when it is often insufficient. Thus, monitoring and measuring activities are important indications of management commitment to health and safety and an essential part of a positive health and safety culture (Lindsay, 1992).

According to Frick (2011), regarding the reduction of accidents, systematic violations of legal requirements has repeatedly caused accidents at workplaces with certified management systems. When employers introduce management systems, it can affect their implementation and outcomes.

Internal objectives of productivity and/or work-related health require upstream prevention and a genuine influence by workers and their safety representatives. It can be concluded that the causes of most occupational accidents in the construction industry are largely due to management negligence or inadequate worker safety awareness (Cheng et al., 2010). Therefore, we can say that when workers are warned of the dangers and are required to comply with laws, they are less negligent which results in fewer accidents and professional illness. It has been concluded from this study that this can be achieved with certification through OHSMS. On other hand, various authors attribute weak management commitment to the general belief that preventive measures require expenditures that have nothing to do with the firm's production objectives (Fernández-Muñiz et al., 2009). Consequently, this negligence can have negative repercussions to profitability and competitiveness. Accidents have adverse effects on decreasing productivity and quality which can result in deterioration of the firm's public image or internal wellbeing. It is for this reason that a good occupational safety management program can have a positive effect, not only on accident rates but also on competitiveness variables and financial performance. This outcome is consistent with this study, particularly regarding the difficulties in changing company culture, lowering the number of accidents, reducing costs of accidents, and occupational diseases, as well as the improvement of company image in the market and community. Moreover, it appears that improvement of the company's image and the increasing numbers of suggestions from employees are practices which bring about the most effective changes. There is an ongoing discussion in the occupational health and safety community about small enterprises – especially those with less than 50 employees. It is generally recognized that these enterprises constitute a special problem with regard to prevention of occupational injuries (Hasle et al., 2009). Any safety management system is a social system wholly reliant upon the employees who operate it (Lee, 2000). Its success depends on three things: its scope, employees' knowledge of it, and whether employees are committed to making it work. The concept of safety culture has evolved as a way of formulating and addressing this new focus. Organizations may also adopt health and safety management systems in order to manage external pressures and at the same time maintain the same internal structures (Granerud and Rocha, 2011).

In Thailand, it seems that most exporter businesses comply with almost all local and some international law, because they have been forced to by their customers (Kongtip et al., 2008). Seen from this perspective, OHSMS certification is just another element in the swarm of novel demands being imposed on firms by external stakeholders. In some cases, an OHSAS 18001 certification could be a prerequisite for gaining contracts from leading firms or for recruiting employees who are in high demand in the general labor market. Some firms even take the next step and deliberately enter competitions to be nominated as the "Best Workplace of the Year" or "Best Place for Apprenticeship," etc., in the same manner as they would compete to win a quality or design prize (Kristensen, 2011). All companies in this study were ISO 9001 certified. Vinodkumar and Bhasi (2011) stated ISO 9001 certified firms have higher levels in all safety management practices except safety promotion policies. It is an important finding that non-certified firms have higher levels of safety promotion policies, even though insignificant when compared with ISO 9001 certified firms. On other hand, considering the Integrated Management Systems (IMS)-QES in Portuguese Companies, it was fundamental to carefully carry out surveys and analyses, namely at the level of the development of the company's Management Sub-systems - OHSMS, EMS, and QMS and to characterize the level of integration and/or potential relationship between them, (the OHSAS 18001, the ISO 14001, the ISO 9001, the ISO 9000:2005, ISO 9004:2011 standards, among others), and to identify common requirements and domains as well as the similarities between them. The observed integration level is also in line with Badreddine et al. (2009), since the use of risk management, as an integrating factor, increases the compatibility and the coordination between the three systems in order to reduce additional problems issued from parallel implementations. There are many models for IMS-QES. The findings of the case study are in line with Asif (2011), when he suggests that, among the organizational changes accompanied by integration, development of lean processes is the most important. In fact, observed integration levels presented in this chapter were developed based upon the Lean Philosophy.

The observed integration level for an IMS, in accordance with DS 8001:2005, is mentioned by Jørgensen (2008) and the observed integration level presented in this chapter is in line with his research. However, various IMS models are referenced or presented by other authors, such as Arifin et al. (2009) and Santos et al. (2011). According to Rasmussen (2007), the common elements/requirements of the different standards may be identified using ISO Guide 72:2001. This was also considered in PAS 99:2012, the model which is recommended for an integrated management structure which is configured with the six main requirements of ISO Guide 72: policy, planning, implementation and operation, performance assessment, improvement and management review, and following the *PDCAI* cycle. Therefore, table B.1 in

Annex B of ISO Guide 72 identifies common management system requirements in ISO standards, which are structured/grouped into six components: B1 – Policy, B2- Planning, B3 – Implementation and Operation, B4 – Performance assessment, B5 – Improvement, and B6 – Management review. The guide recommends that this common structure be followed when developing and reviewing management system standards in order to guarantee their compatibility and to improve their alignment. This was our main concern when presenting the structure of the IMS_QES presented in this chapter.

CONCLUSION

This chapter thoroughly explore and analyze the benefits arising from the implementation of an OHSMS certification after receiving the QMS certification on Portuguese SMEs performance, as well as the observed integration level of management systems, quality, environment, and safety in a company case study. The main benefits identified from OHSMS certification were the "improvement of working conditions" (91.6%), "ensuring compliance with legislation" (83.3%) and "better internal communication for worker about the risks and hazards" (75%). This contribute to a reduction in the number of accidents and their associated costs (58.3%), which provides impetus for improving the company's image in the surrounding area and among customers (33.3%), as well as increasing profitability.

The main difficulties uncovered, in relation to OHSMS certification, can be ascribed to difficulties in changing company culture and high certification costs. With respect to health and safety at work, there is still a lot to do in Portugal and other countries. Several Portuguese SMEs have already implemented the OHSMS and others will follow, mainly, because money can't pay for a human life or a severe disability which lasts the rest of a worker's life. On the other hand, there is no an international ISO standard with a specific structural model for Integrated Management Systems of Occupational, Health and Safety with Environment and Quality, or for other management areas.

The main motivating factors extracted from the internal investigation at the Portuguese Company under study included rationalization and optimization of resources, reduction of costs and bureaucracy, and increasing competitiveness. Several other benefits and difficulties could be highlighted in the context of the development of the integration of quality, environment, and safety certification.

The structure of the integration model for quality, environment, and safety represent added value both in the present and, fundamentally, for the future, not only for the company for which the case study was presented, but also for other organizations by whom it could be adopted, as well as for a whole range of associated stakeholders.

There is plenty of work to be done in the area of the integration of individual management systems, considering the redundancies across the related Management Systems (MSs), and the fact that nowadays there are innumerous. The results indicate that there is still a lot to do in Portugal regarding this field.

MSs for individual systems and new ones are going to appear. In fact, if the requirements of the several MSs are combined and included in a global IMS, the company may promote market leadership and, consequently, improve the sustainability of its business.

ACKNOWLEDGMENT

The authors thank all Portuguese SMEs that answered the questionnaire as well as all their collaborators involved in the performed cases studies. The authors manifest a full acknowledgement to the Journal of Cleaner Production for permission to publish figure 1, the Safety Science for permission to publish figure 2 and Total Quality Management & Business Excellence for permission to publish figures 3 and 4. All figures designed by the authors of this chapter were previously published in the cited journals.

REFERENCES

Arifin, K., Aiyub, K., Awang, A., Jahi, J. M., Iten, R. (2009) - Implementation of Integrated Management System in Malaysia: The Level of Organization's Understanding and Awareness. *European Journal of Scientific Research*. ISSN 1450-216X; Vol.31 No.2:188-195.

Arocena, P., Nunez, 1., Villanueva, M. (2008). The impact of prevention measures and organisational factors on occupational injuries. *Safety Science* 46, 1369–1384.

Asif, M., Searcy, C., Zutshi, A., Fisscher, O. A. M. (2011). An integrated management systems approach to corporate social responsibility. *Journal of Cleaner Production* 56, 7-17.

Block, M. R., Marash, I. R. (2002*). Integrating ISO 14001 into a Quality Management System*. ASQ – Second edition, Milwaukee.

Bottani, E., Monica, L., Vignali, G., (2009). Safety management systems: Performance differences between adopters and non-adopters. *Safety Science* 47, 155–162.

Badreddine, A., Romdhane, T. B., Amor, N. B, (2009). A New Process-Based Approach for Implementing an Integrated Management System: Quality, Security, Environment. In: *Proceedings of the International Multi Conference of Engineers and Computer Scientists, vol. II. IMECS, Hong Kong*.

Casadesus, M., Marimon, F., Inaki Heras, H. (2008). ISO 14001 diffusion after the success of the ISO 9001 model. *Journal of Cleaner Production* 16, 1741 – 1754.

Cheng, C., Leu, S., Lin, C., Fan, C. (2010). Characteristic analysis of occupational accidents at small construction enterprises. *Safety Science* 48, 698–707.

Choudhry, R. M., Fang, D., Mohamed, S. (2007). The nature of safety culture: A survey of the state-of-the-art. *Safety Science* 45, 993–1012.

DS 8001: (2005) – *Integrated management systems* – Approval date – 11 July.

European Agency for Safety and Health at Work. (2002). New Trends in Accident Prevention Due to the Changing World of Work. Report. Luxembourg: Office for Official Publications of the European Communities. Available from: *https://osha.europa.eu/en/publications/reports/208*.

Fernández-Muñiz, B., Montes-Peón, J. M., Vázquez-Ordás, C. J. (2007). Safety culture: Analysis of the causal relationships between its key dimensions. *Journal of Safety Research* 38, 627–64.

Fernández-Muñiz B, Montes-Peón J M, Vázquez-Ordás, C J (2009). Relation between occupational safety management and firm performance. *Safety Science* 47, 980–991.

Fresner, J., Engelhardt, G. (2004). Experiences with integrated management systems for two small companies in Austria. *Journal of Cleaner Production,* Vol. 12, pp. 623-631.

Frick, K. (2011). Worker influence on voluntary OHS management systems – A review of its ends and means. *Safety Science* 49, 974–987.

Fryxell, G. E., Szeto, A. (2002). The influence of motivations for seeking ISO 14001 certification: an empirical study of ISO 14001 certified facilities in *Hong Kong Journal of Environmental Management* 65, 223–238.

González, Eusebio Rial (2012). *The future of OSH in the European Union -10º congresso internacional de segurança e saúde no trabalho*. Porto

Granerud, L., Rocha, R. S., (2011). Organizational learning and continuous improvement of health and safety in certified manufacturers. *Safety Science* 49, 1030–1039.

Guide ISO 72:2001 – *Guidelines for justification and development of management System standards*.

Hasle, P., Bo, B., Granerud, L. (2009). Small enterprises – Accountants as occupational health and safety intermediaries. *Safety Science* 48, 404-409.

Herrero, S. G., Saldana, M. A. M., Campo, M. A. M., Ritzel, D. O. (2002). From the traditional concept of safety management to safety integrated with quality. *Journal of Safety Research* 33, 1 – 20.

ISO (2008). *The integrated use of management system standards*. ISBN 978-92-67-10473-7. Geneva, Switzerland.

Jørgensen, T. H., Remmen, A., Mellado, M. D. (2006). Integrated management systems - three different levels of integration. *Journal of Cleaner Production* 14, 713 – 722.

Jørgensen, T. H. (2008). Towards more sustainable management systems: through life cycle management and integration, *Journal of Cleaner Production* 16, 1071 -1080.

Karapetrovic, S., Casadesús, M. (2009). Implementing environmental with other standardized management systems: Scope, sequence, time and integration. *Journal of Cleaner Production* 17. 533–540.

Kongtip, P., Yoosook, W., Chantanakul, S. (2008). Occupational health and safety management in small and medium-sized enterprises: An overview of the situation in Thailand. *Safety Science* 46, 1356–1368.

Koukoulaki, T. (2010). New trends in work environment – New effects on safety. *Safety Science* 48, 936–942.

Kristensen, P. H. (2011). Managing OHS: A route to a new negotiating order in high-performance work organizations? *Safety Science* 49, 964–973.

Kwon, D. M., Seo, M. S., Seo, Y. C. (2002). A study of compliance with environmental regulations of ISO 14001 certified companies. *Korea Journal of Environmental Management* 65, 347-353.

Lindsay, F. D. (1992). Successful health and safety management. The contribution of management audit. *Safety Science* 15, 387-402.

Mendes, F., Santos, G. (2009). Impacto de la certificacion de los sistemas integrados de gestion en las PMEs portuguesas. *Forum Calidad nº* 198, 46-51.

Mendes, F. (2007). *The Impact of QES systems in Portuguese SMEs.* Master Thesis e Univ. Minho.

Mossink, J. (2002). Inventory of Socio economics Costs of Work Accidents. *European Agency for Safety and Health at Work,* Luxembourg.

PAS 99:2012 – *Publicly available specification - Specification of common management system requirements as a framework for integration.* Second Edition, September 2012. London: BSI – British Standards Limited ISBN: 978-0-580-76869-9.

Piore, M., Sabel, C. F. (1984). *The second industrial divide.* Possibilities for prosperity. Basic Books, New York.

Power, M. (2008). *Organized Uncertainty: Designing a World of Risk Management.* Oxford University Press, Oxford.

Rasmussen, J. M. (2007). *Integrated Management Systems – An Analysis of Best Practice in Danish Companies.* Master Thesis, Aalborg University.

Rebelo, M. F. (2011). *Contribution to the structuring of a model of integrated management system QES.* Master Thesis. Polytechnic Institute Cavado Ave. Portugal.

Roberge, C. L. (1999). It's all about attitude. *Industrial Distribution,* 88 (5), 122.

Robson, L. S., Clarke, J. A., Cullen, K., Bielecky, A., Severin, C., Bigelow, P. L., Irvin, E., Culyer, A., Mahood, Q. (2007). The effectiveness of occupational health and safety management system interventions: A systematic review. *Safety Science* 45, 329–353.

Salomone, R. (2008). Integrated management systems: experiences in Italian organizations, *Journal of Cleaner Production,* 16: 1786 -1806.

Santos, G. (2002). The suggestions process in the continuous improvement of quality. *2ª Engineering Polytechnical.* Setúbal, Portugal.

Santos, G., Ramos, D., Almeida, L., Rebelo, M.F., Pereira, M., Barros, S., & Vale, P. (2013). *Integrated Management Systems: Quality, Environment and Safety.* 2nd Edition. ISBN: 978-989-723-038-7. Publindústria, Edições Técnicas.

Santos, G., Mendes, F., Barbosa, J. (2011). Certification and integration of management systems: the experience of Portuguese small and medium enterprises, *Journal of Cleaner Production* 19, 1965 -1974.

Santos, G., Alves, S., Mendes, F., Lopes, N .(2012). The main benefits associated with Health and Safety Management Systems certification in Portuguese Small and Medium Enterprises post Quality Management System certification. *Safety Science*, 51, 29-36.

Shapiro, R. (2008). *Futurecast*. Portuguese edition, Actual editor (Sept. 2010). ISBN 978-989-8101-79-2.

Simon, A., Karapetrovic, S., Casadesus, M. (2012). Evolution of Integrated Management Systems in Spanish firms. *Journal of Cleaner Production* 23, 8-19.

Sørensen, O. H., Hasle, P., Bach, E. (2007). Working in small enterprises – Is there a special risk? *Safety Science* 45, 1044–1059.

Suditu, C. (2007). Positive and negative aspects regarding the implementation of an integrated Quality, Environment, health and Safety Management System. *Annals of the Oradea University, - Fascicle of Management and Technological Engineering*, Volume VI (XVI).

Tsai, W. H., Chou, W. H. (2009). Selecting management systems for sustainable development in SMEs: A novel hybrid model based on DEMATEL, ANP, and ZOGP. *Expert Systems with Applications* 36, 1444–58.

Tarí, J. J., Molina-Azorín, J. F. (2010). Integration of quality management and environmental management systems Similarities and the role of the EFQM model *The TQM Journal* Vol. 22 No. 6, pp. 687-701.

Vassie, L., Cox, S. (1998). Small and Medium Size Enterprises (SME) interest in voluntary certification schemes for health and safety management: preliminary results. *Safety Science* 29, 67-73.

Vinodkumar, M. N., Bhasi, M. (2011). A study on the impact of management system certification on safety management. *Safety Science* 49, 498–507.

Wright, T. (2000). IMS-Three into One Will Go!: The Advantages of a Single Integrated Quality, Health and Safety, and Environmental Management System. *The Quality Assurance Journal*; 4: 137–42.

Zeng, S. X., Jonathan, J. S., Lou, G. X. (2007). A synergetic model for implementing an integrated management system: an empirical study in China. *Journal of Cleaner Production* 15, 1760 -1767.

Zorpas, A. (2010). Environmental management systems as sustainable tools in the way of life for the SMEs and VSMEs. *Bioresource Technology* 101, 1544 -1557.

INDEX

C

D

Q

R

S

T